FELONS of HATHERSAGE

(a brief history of crime)

David Moseley

FELONS of HATHERSAGE
(a brief history of crime)

David Moseley

Copyright © David Moseley 2021

Second print run 2021

ISBN: 978-1-9196031-1-7

Written by David Moseley and published by Picklecombe Press in association with Writersworld, this book is produced entirely in the UK, is available to order from most book shops in the United Kingdom, and is globally available via UK-based Internet book retailers.

Cover Design: Jag Lall

Cover image: advertising poster from 1863

Copy editor: Sue Croft

WRITERSWORLD
2 Bear Close, Woodstock,
Oxfordshire
OX20 1JX
United Kingdom

www.writersworld.co.uk

The text pages of this book are produced via an independent certification process that ensures the trees from which the paper is produced comes from well managed sources that exclude the risk of using illegally logged timber while leaving options to use post-consumer recycled paper as well.

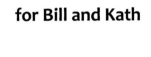

for Bill and Kath

Acknowledgements

A book such as this would not be possible without 240 years of note-keeping by the various secretaries of Hathersage Association for the Prosecution of Felons, and for the care taken to preserve their records over the years.

The glue which was used to stick these snippets together came from two theses which were submitted to the University of Leicester for the award of postgraduate degrees:

- o Family and Community in a Small Industrial Town: Hathersage in the Nineteenth Century
  by Christopher Side, 2018
- o Leaden Heels and Iron Hands: Prosecution Organisations in Derbyshire 1703-2013
  by Robert Mee, 2013

Thanks also go to Heather Rodgers and Michael Shuttleworth for sharing their inside knowledge of Hathersage.

Any profits from the sale of this book will go to Hathersage Association for the Prosecution of Felons and will, in turn, be donated to the local charities which the Association supports: these charities include Edale Mountain Rescue; the Air Ambulance; Helen's Trust; Bakewell & Eyam Community Transport; and Cardiac Risk in the Young.

Contents

Appendices

Front cover: village poster from 1863

Introduction

Hathersage Association for the Prosecution of Felons and Other Offenders was formed in 1784 and continues in existence today. The name sounds like something invented by the Monty Python team, but it describes the original role of the society perfectly. It was a case of something doing exactly 'what it says on the tin'.

Hathersage is a Derbyshire village which is closer to Sheffield than it is to Derby or Manchester, and now increasingly serves as a dormitory for people who work elsewhere. It is also a mecca for climbers, walkers, and cyclists: there are more outlets for the purchase of expensive walking jackets than for buying a tin of beans. But in the past, it was a small industrial township with several factories where wire, needles, and buttons were manufactured, and where children could be exploited while their parents were contracting silicosis. This industrial past is betrayed by such names as Mill Lane, Barnfield Works, Dale Mill, and Millbank Court.

Prosecution associations were a national phenomenon and Hathersage can lay no claim to originality. They were one way in which crime was controlled at a time when police forces had yet to be introduced. Their history is one of local initiatives which were taken to deal with local problems and deserve to be recognized as an early example of localism in action.

The Hathersage Association is one of a few dozen surviving prosecution associations out of an estimated 4,000 such groups which existed in England at one time or another. Those remaining have survived by evolving and adapting to changes in society; they now function as convivial groups of members who enjoy each other's company, and in some cases raise money for local charitable causes. Paradoxically, but for the sake of brevity, they tend to refer to themselves as 'The Felons'.

The records of the Hathersage Association have never been thoroughly interrogated and documented before. This book includes images of many original documents which have barely seen the light of day since they were written, but they represent only a small fraction of those which have been stored for over two centuries and which are often no more than scraps of paper. Some images are accompanied by transcriptions to help in their interpretation, but others have been left for the reader to have the pleasure of interpreting the raw original.

Much of this drama is set in the 19th century, when the industrial revolution was in full swing and persisting social divisions made minor crime a fact of life. But before the action starts, the stage needs to be set within the national context, and we ought to familiarise ourselves with the Hathersage characters who are to play the major roles.

It is hoped that this little book can illuminate some less-familiar aspects of the village's history by shining a light from the unusual direction of minor crime and antisocial behaviour.

Setting the Scene

The English system of criminal justice in the seventeenth and eighteenth centuries was unique. Responsibility for the prosecution of a crime rested with the individual victim of the offence. Unlike in many countries, there was no centralised agency to take on the role of prosecutor.

Each parish had a constable who had a duty to apprehend anyone committing a felony and deliver them to the court, with discretionary powers in lesser cases. He was typically appointed by the local magistrates and his post was unsalaried. He would normally only act on specific requests, and the victim of a crime was responsible for his expenses and any subsequent court costs. As most cases were heard by the county magistrates, either sitting alone or at the quarter sessions, law-enforcement was a very local concern.

There was often a reluctance on the part of victims to carry a case through to court because of the costs involved, so towards the end of the 17th century various incentives for victims to prosecute were introduced. The state offered allowances to assist in prosecuting certain categories of offence such as highway robbery, counterfeiting, and the theft of horses, cattle, or sheep. These were all tried at assizes and were capital offences. But this did nothing to help with the job of prosecuting those people committing the more minor crimes and antisocial behaviour.

Local initiatives, called parish agreements, sprang up across the country in the first half of the 18th century, where ratepayers collectively agreed to their parish paying the cost of prosecution for the minor offences committed within its boundary. The funds for these payments were raised by a levy on the ratepayers, who were by definition members of the property-owning layer of the community. Nonetheless, the system continued to rely on the role of the parish constable.

The earliest parish agreement in Derbyshire was signed on the 7th of February 1740, and it was in Hathersage that twenty-seven ratepayers agreed that all prosecutions for offences committed in the parish would be publicly funded. There was no stipulation in the Hathersage parish agreement that victims needed to be fellow ratepayers in order to qualify for this financial support, and such munificence towards the rest of their community was not universally popular among those who paid the rates. Consequently, the agreement in Hathersage was short-lived, as was the case for most parish agreements.

In 1752, another attempt to incentivize prosecutions saw the courts given powers to order county treasurers to pay victims of the commoner minor crimes '*such sum as was thought reasonable in compensation for the expense, loss of time, and the trouble incurred in carrying on the prosecution*'. However, these payments were dependent on a successful prosecution, which was not guaranteed, and the amount awarded was discretionary and unreliable. The risks of ending up out of pocket continued to dissuade many victims from proceeding down the line of legal action.

The incentives were extended in 1778 to give an allowance to any witness, regardless of their financial position, and to pay prosecutors' costs even if the prosecution failed. And then, in 1783, Derbyshire took a significant further step when the

Quarter Sessions directed that *'in all future Prosecutions for Felonies, the reasonable Charges of the Prosecutors and their Witnesses will be paid by the County'*. This meant that all victims would now receive an allowance from the Derbyshire treasurer. Clearly, this should have opened the door for victims to seek justice, but unfortunately the amount of the allowance seldom seems to have covered the full costs incurred.

All these improvements to the court expenses system were primarily designed to help and encourage the least wealthy victims to pursue prosecutions. But the changes also benefited people who were slightly better off and placed them in a good position to recoup some of their costs too. This improved the feasibility of *independent cooperatives* which could pursue prosecutions for their members and make up the difference out of their common pots whenever the county allowance fell short.

By far the most common form of cooperative was the 'subscription association' model which involved members paying a fee to join, the accumulated cash then being used to fund rewards to witnesses and to subsidise the rest of the prosecution process. After the joining fee, any subsequent payments varied. Either regular monthly or annual subscriptions were made, or additional payments were levied as they were needed. But this fashion for the 'subscription association' model inevitably restricted the protection offered to those people who were willing and able to pay for the privilege of membership and excluded those who weren't or couldn't.

These associations began to be formed throughout England, with those in Essex starting in the 1770s. They represented an attempt by men of property to overcome the perceived deficiencies of the state's law enforcement apparatus and to ensure that their property was better protected. It is estimated that by the end of the 1700s there were around 4,000 such groups in the country.

There was a suspicion that this movement represented an attempt to undermine the existing national system, but the membership base of these groups was made up of landowners, clergy, and lawyers, which suggests that subversion was probably not their objective. The members of the associations appear to have tried to work within the existing system, but they undoubtedly also aimed to improve it. The routine business of the associations was not major crime; rather they served as forums for discussion on the more commonplace local problems which affected the members and their communities. They generally seem to have regarded their mission as crime deterrence rather than an increase in prosecutions.

Rural groups tended to be made up of local landowners and people higher in the social hierarchy; few of the poorer inhabitants joined. It may be that some members benefited from the element of respectability which membership conferred. As well as maintaining their primary declared function, the associations provided a useful method of socialising and networking. Some associations kept their social activities separate from the business of law enforcement, but the accounts of others show that they were intertwined from the outset.

The important decision by the Quarter Sessions in 1783 appears to have been the catalyst for the establishment of the prosecution associations which began to spring up throughout Derbyshire. Within 30 years, most of Derbyshire, except for the more sparsely populated areas and the industrial and coal-mining centres in the north-east of the county, was covered by an association, and those industrial areas went on to form their own collaboratives after 1820. A total of 145 such groups are known to have existed in Derbyshire at one time or another. Hathersage, with a population of about 800 at the time, was relatively quick off the mark, setting up their association in 1784.

Although most of the Derbyshire associations restricted membership to people who were resident in a single parish, in reality they were independent of parish structure and had the ability to define their own geographic boundaries. Hathersage did just that and included a few members from further along the Hope Valley.

Some Notable 19th Century Members

A handful of citizens in Hathersage grasped the significance of the 1783 decision at Derbyshire Quarter Sessions and set about recruiting support for a prosecution association. When a list of villagers who were instrumental in establishing and running the Hathersage Association in the first few years is pulled together, the catalogue reads like a 19th century 'Who's Who' for the village.

Henry Ibbotson was the first name on the 1784 Articles of the Association (Appendix i). Two years later there were four subscribers called Ibbotson and by the end of the 19th century there had been fourteen members with that surname. The Ibbotsons were one of the largest and wealthiest farming families in Hathersage during the 18th and 19th centuries, and they were also long-livers. An article about the family appeared in the *Derby Mercury* in August 1837 claiming that there were six Ibbotson brothers in Hathersage aged between 74 and 90 and that one was still working as a tax collector. *'Nowhere else in the country can match this rare instance of health and longevity in one family'* boasted the newspaper.

The Ibbotsons originated in Hope, moved to Netherhurst, and owned many properties and extensive farming land below Stanage Edge, from Bamford in the west to Greens House in the east. They also dabbled in wire drawing and were instrumental in starting the Globe Steel Works in Sheffield, which remains well-preserved at the bottom of Penistone Road. The Ibbotson name virtually disappears from membership lists of the Association after Victorian times, with just one member in the 20th century.

Another prominent surname throughout the existence of the Association is that of Shuttleworth. The family owned Hathersage Hall and Nether Hall in addition to many acres of farmland, quarries, and lead mines. In 1748 William Shuttleworth, a Captain in the 7th Royal Fusiliers, married Christiana Spencer of Cannon Hall near Barnsley, whose family owned the land in Hathersage, and the couple moved to live at Hathersage Hall. When he died in 1780 the property passed to his nephew, **James Shuttleworth**. James' signature is one of the earliest on the list of 1784 and he remained a member until his death eleven years later.

James Shuttleworth (courtesy of the Shuttleworth family)

Ashton Ashton Shuttleworth joined the Association in 1796 after James died. Ashton has been a common first name for the Shuttleworths after the surname came into the family by marriage, and at that time double-naming was fashionable. Ashton had retired from a distinguished military career. Having been in North America at the outbreak of the War of Independence, he fought at the key battles of Lexington, Bunker Hill, and Brandywine Creek. But in 1796, at the age of 42, his health was not good. He was discharged from the army, came to live at Hathersage Hall, joined the Association for the Prosecution of Felons, and lived for another 34 years.

More than 200 years have passed since then and the name of Shuttleworth has never disappeared from the list, eight members of the family having graced the membership during that time. Some have been Justices of the Peace, several have held senior military rank, and all have been active participants in the Association. One imagines that the 19th century Shuttleworths were keen to protect their property through membership of a prosecution association, but they also took an interest in the village and gave their time to serve the wider community.

A surname which recurs throughout the 19th century is that of Cocker. The Cockers formed a dynasty of wire and needle manufacturers, and **Robert Cocker** was one of the names on the 1786 list of subscribers. He was the son of Solomon Cocker, who arrived in Hathersage from Bamford soon after he got married in 1724. A trained wiredrawer, it was Solomon who initiated the chain of events which led to wire manufacturing becoming such a significant activity in the early 1800s and which was to provide employment in the village for over a century.

Wire had long been used in the manufacture of animal cages and in sieves for grading metal ores, but the number of its uses was increasing. It was in demand for haulage and mooring cables, and in mine-head gear. The first modern suspension bridges were being created at about this time, structures which demanded high quality steel cable.

Robert lived at Carr Head. His son **Thomas** followed his father into the Hathersage Association in 1796, and three of Thomas's sons, **Henry, Samuel**, and **Joseph**, became members in 1809, 1819, and 1856. Henry's son Robert also joined in 1831. A total of seven Cockers, from four generations, were involved with the Association for the Prosecution of Felons at one time or another. Their businesses operated out of Dale Mill and the Atlas Works, which was across the road from the bottom of Jaggers Lane and was demolished in 1907 after being disused for several years.

The Cockers came from a humble background but made a lot of money very quickly towards the end of the 1700s. They worked hard at climbing the social ladder, giving conspicuously to good causes and taking a prominent role in religious and political activities. They intermarried with families such as the Broomheads and the Ibbotsons, who were already high in the village social scale. A Cocker married an Ibbotson on at least five occasions. Membership of the Association for the Prosecution of Felons no doubt also contributed to their reputation for respectability.

Henry Cocker lived at Moorseats and was in the third generation of successful Cockers. His activities spread beyond light engineering. He attended and presented at the Literary and Philosophical Society and was elected to the Royal

Agricultural Society. Unfortunately, Henry was forced into bankruptcy by the collapse of the Parker, Shore & Co Bank in Sheffield. The Corn Laws had caused difficulties in manufacturing and trade, and the Hathersage needle-making industry began to collapse, probably accelerated by the lack of a railway link until almost the end of the century. The whole edifice had tumbled by the 1890s and John, the last of the Cockers, died at the age of thirty-five without producing an heir.

Robert Cook moved into the area from the needle-manufacturing town of Studley in Warwickshire while in his teens. He leased a property from Ashton Shuttleworth in the 1820s which was to become the Barnfield Works. By the time he joined the Association in 1844, the business partnership with his son was well established, manufacturing hackle and gill pins. These were devices which were fabricated from steel wire and used in the textile industry. Hackle pins were short, stiff, bent wires which were set in a wooden board and were so called because they were thought to resemble the hackles of an angry dog. They were used in carding wool or combing flax to split and straighten the fibres and to remove impurities. Gill pins were used for drawing jute, hemp, or woollen textiles. Barnfield also manufactured fishhooks, and towards the end of its existence it made needles for the recently invented gramophone.

For most of the 1830s Robert Cook held the tenancy of the Ordnance Arms (later the Hathersage Inn and now an outdoor equipment store). It had been built as a coaching inn in 1808 by Ashton Shuttleworth in anticipation of a new section of the Sparrowpit Turnpike road coming through the village. It may appear strange to us that a needle manufacturer like Cook, and later Tobias Child, should want to run an inn, but it can be explained by the commerce which went on there: payments for wire or needles and exchange of half-finished products. Perhaps it was his inexperience in running an inn which led to him appearing in court in 1833, accused of causing a stench by leaving his waste and refuse in the street outside the Ordnance Arms.

Robert Cook's sons **Richard** and **James** both joined the Hathersage Association when their father died in 1867, and **John Francis Cook** joined in 1892.

The Cooks' needle business was in direct competition with that of the Cockers. They were newcomers and Catholics, whereas the Cockers had been in the village for a few generations and were Liberals and devout Wesleyans. In the mid-1800s, the numbers of baptisms in the Catholic and Protestant churches in Hathersage were roughly equal and there is no real evidence that the mill owners favoured employing members of their own churches. Although there was probably little love lost between the Cooks and the Cockers, their Association memberships coincided and there are many minutes which record them attending the same small committee meetings. However, the animosity was to boil over into violence at one stage, as we shall see.

There were also major disputes within the Cook family itself. Robert had a reputation as an awkward man to deal with and from various records he appears to have frequently conducted himself in a confrontational manner. Even the Catholic priest went on record to describe him as 'a very strange man to have anything to do with'. He was less popular in the village than the Cockers, and there was the occasional walk-out by his workers. The Barnfield business began to contract in the 1860s and failed at around the same time as that of the Cockers. Whereas it could be argued that the failure of the Cocker family's Dale Mill and Atlas Works was due to misfortune, the failure of the Cook family's Barnfield business seems to have been more to do with conflict and mismanagement.

Tobias Child was born in 1805 in Darlington and moved to live in Hathersage while still in his teens. He was initially involved in farming, but became a sufficiently close friend of wire-maker Thomas Cocker to be a witness to Cocker's will in 1829, and by 1841 he had leased the Pearson workshops from John Shuttleworth and started his own manufacturing business. The factory was beside the Hood Brook, under the railway arch on Mill Lane, although there was no arch at that time of course. The Pearsons had manufactured calico at the building, but by the time of the 1841 census none of the Hathersage residents was listed as a textile worker, unlike in the villages further along the Hope Valley. Child renamed his factory after the monarch, and what remains of his Victoria Works is now a luxury holiday let. He also took the tenancy of the 'Ordnance Arms' when Robert Cook gave it up in 1838. In the 1851 census he is described as a 'hackle pin manufacturer employing fifteen men and three farm labourers'.

Tobias Child joined the Hathersage Association for the Prosecution of Felons in 1844 and served on the committee for several years. When he was chairman of the committee in 1850, he attempted to get the 2s/6d fine for non-attendance at a meeting changed such that a non-attender would instead send a bottle of wine for consumption by the other members. The idea was never adopted but it is difficult not to admire his style.

Robert Cook and Tobias Child were examples of men who came from what would now be called working-class backgrounds, started manufacturing businesses in Hathersage and thus came into 'new money'. They sought to emulate the gentry by buying rights to shoot on the grouse moors and giving generously to charity. They both happened to join the Association in the same year, 1844. Once again one wonders whether membership of the Association, in addition to offering some protection to their property, represented a networking opportunity which also conferred some recognition and acceptance on the social ladder.

Chris Kirk was a name on the early membership lists. He had built Bamford cotton mill in 1780, but it burned down during the night of 24th of October 1791; he joined the Hathersage Association for the Prosecution of Felons two months later. It is tempting to think that the two events may have been linked, though it was never established that he was the victim of an arsonist. The Luddite movement did not officially begin until 1811, but there was certainly a history of textile workers destroying industrial equipment in the late 1700s.

Just the walls of the mill building survived the blaze, the damage being estimated at £800. Although only insured for £500, he had it rebuilt, presumably stumping up for the shortfall out of his own pocket. Could Chris Kirk have been trying to protect his future interests when he joined the Association? He died in 1822 and membership was taken by his widow, and then son, but the surname disappears from the list of members in 1847.

William Cameron Moore was born in Baltimore. He bought the Bamford Cotton Mill in the 1850s and he also owned a mill in Manchester. He joined the Hathersage Association in 1864 and was a member for 24 years. In addition to being a Justice of the Peace he was a major philanthropist and benefactor within Bamford, funding the building of the school, the church hall, and houses for his workers.

Williamson Art Gallery & Museum, Birkenhead; Wirral Museums Service

Charles Cammell moved to live at Brookfield in Hathersage in 1867 and joined the Association in 1869. He had set up Johnson Cammell and Co. in Sheffield in 1837, developing the Cyclops Steel & Iron Works to make rails, railway equipment, and armoured plate. A year after joining the Association he opened a factory making railway wheels in Dronfield. It was a good business to be in at that time. Charles died in 1879 and the membership passed to his son **George**, who also took over Brookfield, but before George was formally accepted as a member of the Association a 'larceny' was committed at Brookfield by James Winslow. The successful prosecution depended on evidence from George Creesey, and the Association agreed to reward Creesey with one guinea despite Cammell junior not officially having become a member at the time of the offence.

George Cammell, Charles' son, was the man who gave his

surname national fame and remained a member until his death in 1905. His business flourished; their armoured plate was used in a version of mobile weaponry which predated the tank and was used in the Boer War. In 1903, his company merged with Laird Brothers to form Cammell Laird, the huge shipbuilding company on Merseyside, but he still found time to be an active member of the Association and became a Justice of the Peace. He provided the money for a new clock on the tower of Hathersage church in 1879.

Dr Joseph Henry Taylor was born in New Mills in 1821, and by the age of twenty he was working as a surgeon on Town Street in Bradwell. He was still the doctor in Bradwell when in 1865 he joined the Hathersage Association, but by 1880 he was living in Hathersage and had 'The Hollies' built, the house which is now Hathersage Youth Hostel but was then the village's first purpose-built medical facility. Some of the older residents of Hathersage will remember that the lower portion of Jaggers Lane was always known as 'Doctor's Hill'. Dr Taylor was committed to the communities in which he lived, being church

Dr Taylor

warden at the new Bradwell church and serving on Bradwell school's board after the important Education Act of 1870. An ever-present at committee and general meetings of the Hathersage Association, he became its first president in 1890 and continued to practise medicine and take a very active role in the Association right up to his death in 1897.

Dr Lander

Although Dr Taylor was the first medic to be a member of the Association, his successor in the practice at The Hollies, **Dr Herbert Graham Lander**, was immediately elected to membership in 1897. He was another member who appears to have been motivated by a sense of community, but he died suddenly in 1917, at the age of fifty. Due to give a talk at the school, he was found dead in the school yard. There is a plaque to his memory on the wall inside Hathersage church.

The medical practice at The Hollies was then taken over by **Dr William Houlbrook**, the first local doctor in the Hope Valley to drive a motor car. Dr Houlbrook became a member of the Association from 1921 until the start of the Second World War.

The 19th century industrialist members of the Association eventually began to leave the stage. As the Cockers, Cooks, and Cammells made their exits, they were replaced by Crosslands and Thorpes. Joseph Cocker's sale of his share in the organization to **Henry Crossland** marked the end of a century-long link between the Cocker family and the Hathersage Association. His death four years later was the final straw for the Atlas Works, which ceased production soon afterwards and threw scores of Hathersage residents into unemployment.

Receipt from Henry Crossland to Joseph Cocker for his share

From 1875 to the present day there has always been at least one member from the Crossland family in the Association, and three generations of Thorpes have served continuously for the last 116 years.

In addition to the £1-10s which Henry Robert Crossland paid to Joseph Cocker, he would have paid a fee of ten shillings to the Association. Mr Crossland had been born at Birley Farm in Hathersage in 1850, but when he became a member in 1883, he was farming at Nether Padley. His membership of the

Association lasted fifty years and he served as its president for much of that time. He was an Alderman to the county and a Justice of the Peace.

The transfer of a share in the Hathersage Association from a wire mill owner to an alderman farmer could be viewed as a metaphor for the direction in which the village was heading as the 19th century drew to a close.

The Early Years in Hathersage

The original Articles of Agreement in 1784 (Appendix i) are worthy of close scrutiny, as are the redrafted Articles from 1838 (Appendix ii). The 1784 document was drawn up between Henry Ibbotson of Car Head (sic), George Morton of Hathersage, and Richard Oliver of Outlane. These three gentlemen were joined by nine others, who also signed the Agreement when it had been written. The cash book, with the earliest surviving list of monthly subscribers, is dated 1786. By then there were twenty-one names in it, but this was soon whittled down to sixteen as the reality of committing to a monthly payment kicked in.

Most Derbyshire groups held an annual meeting of all their members, normally with a meal at a local inn, but the Hathersage Association started with a monthly 'Clubb night' at which they collected regular subscriptions. The amount varied from month to month in the first few years. For some months it is recorded that each member was asked for a subscription of 6d while for other months the subscription was 2s-6d or even 5 shillings. This higher amount would have meant a monthly contribution equivalent to a modern £35.

The subscriptions were designed to build up a balance in the bank, thus providing an operating capital. The monthly system was abandoned in 1797 and replaced by an annual subscription, with a single annual meeting starting in 1808, always on the last Thursday of each year.

The change from monthly to annual meetings created the

need to elect a small committee of members who were prepared to meet whenever it became necessary to conduct the routine business of prosecuting crimes during the rest of the year. The five committee members were given authority to offer rewards to informants and to reimburse any member who had incurred expenses when pursuing a prosecution. One member rotated off the committee each year.

The role of committee member doesn't appear to have been too unpleasant. The small group would meet in a local inn and their refreshments would be paid for by the Association.

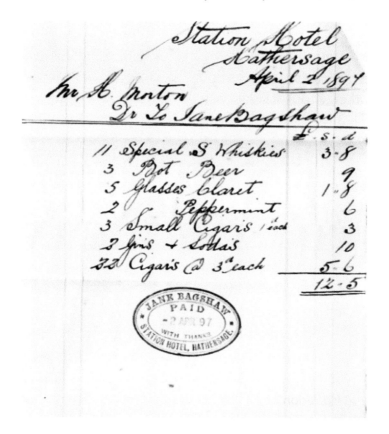

Judging by this earliest surviving detailed invoice submitted to the treasurer by Jane Bagshaw of the Station Hotel (now the Little John) following a committee meeting in 1897, the proceedings must have taken place in a fug of cigar smoke and inebriation. The minutes show that this particular meeting was attended by five members plus the secretary. Mrs Bagshaw was also a member of the Association for a brief time.

The first recorded expenditure on legal proceedings by the Hathersage Association was in 1786, when a total of £13-6s-9d (around £2,000 in today's money) was spent on taking two men to Derby Assizes. Their surnames were Milns and Eyre, but the crime for which they were tried is not detailed in the Association's records. The money went on subpoenas, lawyers' bills, paying the Clerk of the Assizes, travel expenses, and various wages. Later that year £5-15s-7d was spent on warrants and lawyers' bills for prosecuting a man called Cocker. Again, there are no details of his offence.

As most crime was committed by locals, it was felt that the knowledge that a property belonged to a member of the Association would persuade any potential offender to go elsewhere in order to commit their offence. Members were therefore keen to make residents in the close-knit community aware of their membership status and Hathersage, like other associations, printed the names of their members in the local newspaper and on posters in an attempt to deter crime, or at least move it away from their own doorsteps.

In 1801 the Hathersage Association had a hundred handbills printed and posted around local villages to advertise the Association's existence and to list the names of its members. They had fresh posters printed from time to time as the membership changed. While association members clearly believed that having their names published made them less likely to become victims, it remains debatable whether such attempts at displacing crime ever actually worked.

Poster from 1821

Expences attending Tho' Cocker & Sons Robbery

1821

Jan'

5 Warrants _ at 2/-0	10. 0	
To Constables other men	1. 1. 0	
expences to Bakewell ____	0. 7. 3	
Wild 5/- Hobson 5/-____	0. 10. 0	
Expences to Sheffield & Whiteley		
Wood 4 Journeys ____	1. 1. 0	
Printing HandBills ____	0. 11. 6	
2 Chancery cost each 10/6 _	1. 1. 0	
Geo Sheldon 3/- Postage 9d _	0. 3. 9	
	£5. 5. 6	

The typical cost of a prosecution in the early days of the Hathersage Association is illustrated by this slip of paper from 1821, and its transcription. It relates to a robbery at the wire mill owned by Thomas Cocker, who had been a member since 1796. The total amount involved would be worth about £530 now.

The amount in the Hathersage Association's coffers gradually increased because of the annual subscriptions and the accumulation of bank interest. At the AGM in 1841, it was decided to limit the bank balance to £60 (worth about £6,000 today) and anything over that amount was to be put to 'defray the cost of the Annual Feast'.

This "problem" of having too much money in the accounts was solved in 1843 when a Sheffield lawyer called Albert Smith presented a bill to the treasurer for £24 (£2,300 nowadays) after conducting a prosecution of two people who had broken into Hannah Oliver's house. Mrs Oliver had taken over membership following the death of her husband in 1822. Despite the members contesting the lawyer's bill for over a year, it was eventually paid, and the balance in the bank fell to £36. It didn't recover to its previous levels for another forty years.

Because the treasurer of the Association was obliged to make several trips to the bank each year to deposit or withdraw money, he made a claim on the accounts for his expenses each time that he conducted such a journey, and the records show where the money went. For the first few years the money was taken to William Howe in Hope, but by 1827 the trips were being made to Parker, Shore & Co, a large Sheffield bank. Then, by 1840, the journeys had changed again, and the money was being deposited with the Sheffield Banking Company on George Street, near Barkers Pool in Sheffield.

The financial headache that resulted from the lawyer's bill in 1843 could have been much worse. For whatever reason the switch away from Parker Shore was made in 1840, it turned out to be a wise move: the bank went belly up in 1843 and most of its customers lost their money, Henry Cocker being one of them. Had the Hathersage Association still been banking with Parker Shore the bill from Albert Smith would have presented an even bigger headache.

Journeying over the hill between Hathersage and Sheffield by horse came with risks, particularly if you were carrying money, as the treasurer would have been. There were various routes available. The Sparrowpit Turnpike which was developed in the 1700s ran between Sheffield and Stockport. From Hathersage it followed the current route up the Dale, circling around Callow Bank to Overstones, and after Ringinglow going down to Banner Cross. In 1811 the first part of the route was made easier by going up Sheffield Road to The Booths and then branching left at Whim Corner. Another route went via The Surprise, Fox House, and Houndkirk, and there was also the old track via Gatehouse, past Stanage Pole, and onwards to Lodge Moor. All these routes had to cross stretches of open moorland and there are many recorded cases of travellers being assaulted. Fortunately, none of them involved the treasurer, but two incidents serve to illustrate the problem.

In the winter of 1834, by which time Samuel Cocker had been a member of the Association for fifteen years, he was driving his gig back from Sheffield when a large dog tried to stop his horse. He whipped the dog away and carried on, but it followed him. A little further on, two men jumped out of the heather and tried to drag Mr Cocker out of the gig, but the dog attacked the robbers and drove them off. Once order had been restored, the dog continued to follow the gig all the way back to Hathersage. Mr Cocker had never seen it before, but he and his family adopted the animal, which became something of a celebrity in the village. An article describing the incident appeared in the Sheffield newspapers.

Thomas Hodgkinson covered the journey between Fox House and Hathersage twice a day in his job carrying the post, but in 1839 he was assaulted by two men called Abbott and Hancock, who stole his watch and a purse containing £6-16s. He managed to get to the village to raise the alarm. James Cocker, a son of Henry, but about the only Cocker never to be a member of the Association, took eleven handpicked men from Dale Mill and set out onto the moor in pursuit of the culprits. They caught the two robbers, who were taken to court, pleaded guilty and were sentenced to be transported for fifteen years.

It wasn't until 1892 that the treasurer stopped his regular rides over the hill to Sheffield, the Association's account being transferred to the Crompton & Evans Union Bank Limited in Hathersage. This was rather ironic as it was just before the railway link to Sheffield was established in 1894 and the journey would have become easier and safer. On their letterhead, Crompton & Evans described themselves as the 'Scarsdale and High Peak Bank'. As can be seen in the letter from the Sheffield bank, Henry Morton had to make one last journey and bring the cash back across to Hathersage. The bank balance had just recovered by then and the amount that he carried back would have had the spending power today of about £8,000. Modern online banking certainly has some benefits. Although the thieves are still around, they don't need to hide in the heather any more.

Telegraphic Address.
FINANCE, SHEFFIELD

Sheffield Banking Company, Limited.

Sheffield, 5th Jan 1892

Dear Sir,

We shall be glad to pay the amount standing to the credit of the Hathersage association for the Prosecution of Felons any time when it is convenient for you to call.

All that will be necessary is for you to fill up a cheque for the amount, which you can do when you are at the Bank.

Yours faithfully,
Edw Birks
Manager

Henry Marton Esq,
Hathersage.

Letter from Sheffield Banking Co. re payment of the outstanding amount to the Hathersage Association for the Prosecution of Felons

Membership

As of 2021, a total of 262 individuals have been members of the Hathersage Association for the Prosecution of Felons, but there have been periods where people did not retain their membership for long. If we take away those whose membership lasted for five years or less, we are left with 183 historic members over a period approaching 250 years (Appendix iii). John Shuttleworth currently holds the longevity record by being a member for 64 years from 1830.

The sort of people attracted to membership has remained remarkably constant over the years: what one observer has described as 'collectives of mainly middling sorts'. The first five names on the parchment for the 1838 redrafted Articles of Association (Appendix ii) are: William Morton, miller and butcher; Henry Cocker, wire drawer; Charles Ibbotson, farmer; Thomas Broomhead, grocer; Henry Broomhead, shoemaker. There have been clergy: Rev Powell, the Hathersage vicar, joined in 1791; Rev Charles Cutler was a member from 1879, and several Hathersage vicars have taken honorary membership. Although it wasn't until 1865 that the local doctor became a member, the medical profession has been represented three more times since then. On several occasions the local bank manager has been given membership so that he could act as treasurer to the Association.

In her excellent book *Hathersage in the Peak: A History*, Barbara Buxton describes the Association as 'a society of gentlemen devised to keep local order in an age when only a constable maintained the peace'. Most of the current members would struggle to recognise themselves in that description, and while it is not entirely historically accurate either, it is probably close enough.

The list of subscribers in 1786 includes Mary Ibbotson and Fanny Taylor. There have been seven female members over the years, two taking on membership after the deaths of their husbands, who had been members. The last female member was Elizabeth Walker, a widow who ran the George Hotel. Her membership ran for nine years and ended in 1907. For some reason, the Hathersage Association has become a male preserve since then, as have the other associations which survive in the area. So much for us living in more enlightened times.

A few Derbyshire associations chose to maintain an element of exclusivity by limiting their membership. As early as 1808 the Hathersage Association restricted its membership to twenty. This was later raised to twenty-five, but not until 1882. It remains at twenty-five today. For much of its history, membership has been considered a privilege, and it is fair to say that an invitation to join continues to be considered as such. It has been customary to give the first offer of membership to a son of a deceased member. With the exception of a few brief periods of its existence, resignation from the Hathersage Association has not been the norm, nor has it been taken lightly, as is reflected in the letter to the secretary in 1819, which is reproduced on the following page.

The Waltons were a family of malt manufacturers in Hathersage in the late eighteenth century. They rented Hathersage Hall at the time when the Shuttleworths, who owned it by then, were serving overseas with the army. Thomas Walton was an elderly man in 1819 and clearly didn't write the letter himself, but his slightly wobbly signature looks to be by the hand of a frail man. One of the subscribers on the 1786 list, he had been involved with the Association for thirty-three years, and the letter was read out at the Annual Feast in 1819, to the general dismay of the other members.

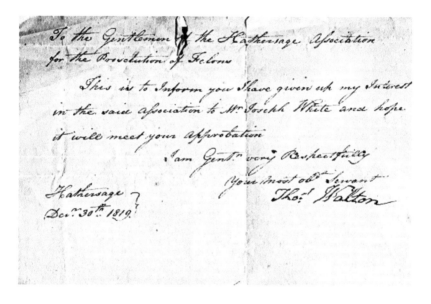

1819 Letter of resignation from
Thomas Walton

John Francis Cook of Barnfield Works sold his membership in 1902 and sought the approval of the Association for Mr Ashmole of Cliffe Cottage to purchase his share and succeed him. This letter marks the end of the Cook family's fifty-eight-year involvement in the Association and was written at the time when their Barnfield business was in terminal decline. John

Cook had only been a member for ten years and Mr Ashmole, his successor, lasted just two. 1902 is also a time when turnover in the membership was unusually high for some reason.

Barnfield,
Hathersage.
Nr. Sheffield.

Dear Sir

Persecution of Titans

I am h/desirous to sell my share in this association to Mr Ashmole of Cliffe Cottage if the members are agreeable for me to do so,

Yours faithfully
John Cook

Henry Morton Esq

Members occasionally defaulted on their subscription or on their fines for non-attendance at meetings. After two years of default a member would automatically forfeit the benefits of membership. In 1830 '*Widow Kirk*' from Brough, a member of the Association, asked for money to keep her servant in custody. The request was denied as Mrs. Kirk had '*not conformed to the rules of our Club*'. To be more precise, from an examination of the accounts, Mrs. Kirk doesn't appear to have been paying her subs for three years.

At a meeting of the Committee for the Prosecution of Fellons in Hathersage held the 4th day of February 1830 to consider an application made by Mrs Kirk of Brough for expenses in keeping in custody her servant gearl on suspicion of a Roberry on the said Mrs Kirk, but finding she has not conformed to the rules of our Club

                             not

we consider it ^ right ~~not~~ to allow them

Any attempt to suggest an individual's motives for joining the Association is inevitably speculation, but the nature of the times, the occupation of a member and the way that they conducted other aspects of their lives can provide some clues. When the Association was formed in the 1780s, we can be sure that most members joined so that their property gained an extra layer of protection from petty criminals. But this hasn't been the case for the past ninety years, when the opportunity to spend sociable evenings with people of a similar mind has been the only reason for taking membership.

Upwardly mobile 19th century wire mill owners may have been interested in the possibility of 'networking' at a time when the term had yet to be invented and when there were fewer opportunities to do so than there are today. On the other hand, a farmer such as George Platts from Nether Hurst, who was also a church warden, is more likely to have had an altruistic motive than a commercial interest.

Right up to the 1970s, members would purchase a 'share' in the organisation from a retiring member or from a deceased member's executors. From the earliest days this share would cost the purchaser two pounds: £1-10s of the payment would go to the seller while a fee of 10 shillings went to the Association. However, if the share was to be inherited within a family there was no fee to be paid. But whether the share was bought or inherited, any new member had to be subjected to a ballot of the other members to ensure their suitability and acceptability.

An interesting problem occurred when Joseph Broomhead died in 1890. He lived at Eastwood, opposite Hathersage church, and had been a member for ten years. His son was a lawyer in Somerset and demanded to know the amount of money in the

Association's bank account and the number of current members. Some simple arithmetic led him to believe that his dead father's share was therefore worth £2-14s-0d. Letters passed in both directions, and interestingly only appear to have taken twenty-four hours to do so. The committee stood its ground. They politely explained that this was not how things were done in Hathersage. Six years later the stand-off was eventually resolved when the share was sold to the new owner of Eastwood, and for the customary amount.

By the end of the 19th century the population of Hathersage was 1200 and rising, as the rail link enabled people who worked in Sheffield to live in the fresh air of a village where the mills were closed or closing. The reputation of the Association was such that in 1899 it was agreed to add up to five honorary members who could enjoy the social benefits but had no voting entitlement. These places occasionally led on to full membership, but the scheme appears to have been dropped soon after the Great War.

Colonel Chadburn was the last honorary member, in 1919. He went on to full membership a year later. He lived at Brookfield and, according to his letterhead, his telephone number was Hathersage 6. The George Hotel's stationary indicates that its phone number was Hathersage 5.

BROOKFIELD MANOR
HATHERSAGE
SHEFFIELD

Jany. 16. 1919.

Dear Sir —

Will you please convey
to the Committee my thanks
for the honour they have done
me in making me an honor.
ary member of the Association
I will have great pleasure
in attending the Dinner on
the 30th.

Yours truly
A. W. Chadburn.

B.M. Heald Esq.

*Letter from Colonel Chadburn thanking the
Association for his honorary membership*

Most of the offences for which rewards were offered over the years involved **theft of livestock**. Frequently it was the thieving of a few poultry (ducks, fowls, and geese), and less commonly of pigeons or sheep. An indication of the penalty which could be expected after conviction for such offences can be gained from the case of Benjamin Hobson. He stole fifteen geese from Anthony Farnsworth of Thorpe Farm in 1838 and was sentenced to four months in Derby prison, complete with hard labour.

HATHERSAGE
Association for the
PROSECUTION OF
FELONS.
FIVE
GUINEAS REWARD.

WHEREAS on the night of September 22nd. or early on the morning of the 23rd., some Person or Persons broke into the FOWL HOUSE of Mr. JOSEPH CROSS-LAND, LEACH HOUSE Hathersage, & stole therefrom a number of Fowls.

NOTICE IS HEREBY GIVEN, that the abovenamed Association offers a Reward of Five Guineas to any person who shall give such information as shall lead to the conviction of the offender or offenders.

By Order of the Committee,

Hathersage Sept. 23rd., 1893.   HENRY MORTON, Secretary.

Any member of the Association who was the victim of a crime needed to contact the secretary within three days of the offence to seek the Association's financial support in taking matters further. The secretary would then call a meeting of the committee 'at his earliest convenience'.

A letter with five signatories makes such a request after sheep were stolen in Grindleford in 1820. Only one of the signatories, William Eyre, was on the list of members at the time, but that was enough for the committee to agree to support the prosecution. In the next chapter we will see the invoices which were subsequently presented to the treasurer for the cost of publicising the reward in this case, both in the newspapers and by bill posting. The identity of the thief was already well known, but the reward was offered to encourage willing witnesses to come forward and stand up in court.

We whose Names are herewith set having had sheep stolen by a Matthew Kay of Grindleford bridg Labourer, and being desirous of bringing the said Matthew Kay to Justice, do agree each for ourselves to be an equal joint reference towards apprehending and prosecuting the offender according to Law __

As witness our hands this first day of March 1820 __

John Hague
Micah Hall
John Oliver
Ab^m Ibbotson
William Eyre

Examination of contemporary newspapers indicate that **horse theft** was a common problem too, although only one theft of a horse is mentioned in all of the Association's papers, presumably because the seriousness of the offence meant that it was dealt with elsewhere. It is easy for us to underestimate the importance of the horse in the 19th century, accustomed as we are to the convenience of the internal combustion engine.

Charles Robinson, who farmed at Crookhills, also ran the Ashopton Inn in the village of Derwent, which, together with the nearby village of Ashopton, was submerged to create the Ladybower Reservoir in the 20th century. Charles had been a member from 1847 and there had been a theft of wool from his barn at Crookhills during the following year. Some geese were also stolen from the farm in a separate incident later in 1848. We now think of Crookhills as being an isolated farmstead with no other homes nearby, and an unlikely spot for casual thieves to take the trouble to visit. But at that time it would have been quite close to the village.

When Charles died in 1867 his membership passed to his widow, and when she died in 1877 it passed on again to his son John. John Robinson was described in the 1881 census as a 'licenced victualler'. He ran the Ordnance Arms in Hathersage and he was the only member who ever asked for help in prosecuting a horse theft after he had a mare stolen from a field at Wood Lane, Ashopton, in 1884. The ancient maps show that Wood Lane was a main road near the centre of the village. A five-guinea reward was offered by the Hathersage Association and John Robinson was encouraged to prosecute, but there is no evidence of that reward ever being claimed nor of a prosecution being brought.

There was a robbery at George Morton's hack yard when a hack cover was stolen. Mr. Morton ran the George Inn and that is where the hack yard was situated. The committee members offered a 10-guinea reward for information leading to a conviction.

Both the George Inn and the Ordnance Arms in the village offered horses for hire throughout the 19th century, in addition to the usual services which could be expected from an inn. This is much the same as our local pub running a car rental business on the side.

Hiring out horses came with potential problems, as we will see in the next chapter, but there was an added benefit too: that of being able to sell the bi-product. Nevertheless, it remains a mystery why the landlord should have invoiced the Association for 5 tons 6½ cwt of manure (at 7s/6d a ton) following the 1883 AGM and Annual Dinner at the George Hotel. There is no mention of manure in the AGM minutes nor in the accounts. The bowl of punch, whisky, and cigars are easier to explain away.

As something of a practical historical diversion, it may be entertaining to consider whether Mr. Marrison was correct when he charged £1-19s-9d for the manure. It will enable older readers to exercise those unused skills which were hammered into their heads at primary school, and for anyone educated after the introduction of decimalisation and metric measures it will offer an insight into to what their parents had to endure for hours on end during childhood. The author's verdict will appear at the end of the chapter.

Theft was common. Thomas Broomhead farmed seventy acres at Eastwood and also had a corn mill and a grocer's shop in the village. In 1845 someone broke into his mill and stole flour. A 10-guinea reward was offered for information.

Oct 21st 1844
At a Meeting of the Committee of the Heatherisage Association for the Prosecution of Felons, it was agreed to offer a reward of Ten Guineas to any person as shall give information on conviction of any Person who broke into the Mill belonging to Thomas Broomhead and Stealing therefrom a quantity of Flour

Then in 1856 the same Mr. Broomhead had his shop broken into and sugar was stolen; on that occasion a 15-guinea reward was offered. Breaking and entering was clearly regarded very seriously as these rewards were at the upper end of the range.

> Anglers Inn, Bamford
> 23 Sept 1893.
>
> Mr H Morton
> Dear Sir
>
> I am under the necessity
> of writing you that I have
> had some pilfering of
> potatoes going on some time
> and I should be glad if the
> Association would take the
> matter up by offering a
> reward for the apprehension
> of the offenders.
> Your kind attention
> will oblige
> Yours Truly
> W Wallworth

William Wallworth of the Anglers Inn in Bamford (presumably now the Anglers Rest), was a member of the Association and in September 1893 he wrote to the secretary to report that there had been some *'pilfering of potatoes going on some time'*. The potato pilfering problem was discussed at the same meeting as the theft of fowls from Leach House that is mentioned in the poster shown at the start of this chapter; a reward of five guineas was offered for each offence. Neither reward was claimed, and both sets of pilferers presumably went unpunished.

A fir tree was stolen from Mr. Shuttleworth's land in 1912. It occurred on December 24th, so it isn't too difficult to make a guess at the thief's motive. The committee displayed some Christmas spirit by offering a reward of only ten shillings for information leading to an arrest, and there is no record of the reward having been claimed. One hopes that it brought the thief's family a happy Christmas.

Some offences were simple **vandalism**. In 1842, Thomas Broomhead's cart was stolen and *'bowled into the brook'* in Hathersage. Fences got broken on Eyam Moor, where John Bagshaw of Highlow had some land in 1859. And when John Shuttleworth had a wall knocked down on Boxing Day 1863, the bizarre financial details of the prosecution show why the monetary help offered by prosecution associations was so necessary in dealing with antisocial behaviour.

Those accused of the pushing over Mr Suttleworth's wall on Boxing Day were William Schofield and Joseph Wilson, who were summoned to appear in front of three magistrates in Bakewell. Schofield didn't turn up and was fined £5-6s and 16s-6d costs in his absence, with the threat of two months in jail if he didn't pay. Wilson did attend the court and was fined £2-12s plus 16s-6d costs, with one month's imprisonment if he failed to pay. 30-year-old George Wiggett from the village was given £1 by the Association as a reward for providing information which led to the convictions. After payment of the above, the actual repair to the damaged wall cost just 6s-0d.

Mr. Shuttleworth was again the victim of vandalism in 1891 and the minutes of a committee meeting in April relate that he had someone 'enter Bolehill Quarry Millstone Edge and commit wilful damage to the millstones and Plant therein'. The Quarry is below the bend in the road at the Surprise and it had been producing grindstones for the cutlery industry and millstones for corn since mediaeval times.

April 15 1891
Dear Sir
I write to call for
a meeting to some wilfull
& malicious damage done
to the Millstones & Plant in
Bole Hill Quarry at Millstone
Edge on Sunday last the
12th inst and I ask that a
Notice be given offering a
Reward to any one who will
give such Evidence as
will convict the offenders
　　　　Yours truly
　　　　John S A Shuttleworth

　　　to Mr Henry Morton

apl. 17. 1891.

J. S. A. Shuttleworth Esq. having given notice that some person or persons did on Sunday the 12th inst. enter Bolehill Quarry Millstone Edge and commit wilful damage to the Millstones & Plant therein A committee meeting was called this day at which it was agreed to offer a reward of Five Guineas to such person as shall give information as shall lead to the conviction of the offender or offenders.

Joseph Crosland. Chairman
C E Harrison
Henry Morton. secty h

Minutes of the meeting at which it was agreed to offer a reward

By the end of the 1800s, imported French stones and the introduction of emery stone were affecting sales; scores of large millstones that had been completed were simply abandoned when the market for them collapsed. They are now only partly obscured by lichen, moss, and bracken. It must have taken a determined effort to damage millstones and a reward of five guineas was offered, but never claimed.

Photo: Alison Moseley

Bolehill quarry was purchased from John Shuttleworth by the Derwent Valley Water Board in 1901 to provide stone for constructing the walls of the Derwent and Howden dams. Over a period of seven years, well over a million tons of stone were cut and transported ten miles up the Derwent Valley.

The green spaces and rock faces in Bolehill Quarry are now favourite haunts for picnickers and rock climbers.

Whether this vandalism to the machinery and millstones in Bolehill Quarry was a case of industrial sabotage is not recorded, but what had happened at Robert Cook's Barnfield Works in December 1889 certainly was. During the workers' dinner break, someone placed a large stone in the cogwheel, which was connected to the main flywheel of the factory. By that time, the system was powered by a 40-horse-power steam engine. The stone was spotted soon after the steam was put back on, although unfortunately not before the main shaft had sheared. This was reported in the *Derby Mercury* as a case of 'rattening', an obsolete northern term for sabotage in an industrial dispute.

The Cooks offered a reward in the *Derby Mercury*, but Robert didn't approach the Association for any financial help. Two similar incidents had happened a few weeks earlier and they may have been an attempt by a worker to introduce the trade union. Although the *Derby Mercury* article declares '*there being no dispute between the master and workpeople*', it was clearly a case of trouble at t'mill.

William Bocking's shop was vandalised in 1899. Mr Bocking was born in Abney in 1860 and opened a grocery store with his wife Delia opposite the Station Hotel (now the Little John) at the bottom of Station Road. Older residents still refer to Oddfellows Row as 'Bocking's Back'. Legend has it that if the Bockings didn't have in stock what a customer wanted, they would go into the back of the shop, nip out of the back door, and fetch the item from the shop across the road. They did their best to keep their customers satisfied!

HATHERSAGE ASSOCIATION FOR THE PROSECUTION OF FELONS, &C.

TWO GUINEAS REWARD.

WHEREAS, on the night of January 9th, some Person or Persons maliciously broke a PLATE GLASS WINDOW in the Shop occupied by Mr. William Bocking, and this Association hereby offers a Reward of Two Guineas to any Person giving such information as shall lead to the conviction of the offender or offenders.

By order of the Committee,

Hathersage, Jan. 11th, 1899.   H. MORTON, Secretary.

W J GREENUP, PRINTER, FLAT STREET, SHEFFIELD.

William Bocking was never a member of the Association, yet a reward was offered because, according to the minutes of the committee meeting, the shop was leased out at the time of the vandalism to Elizabeth Platts, the wife of one of the members. The shop was later taken over by Mr Bocking's son, another William, and was still striving to keep customers satisfied well into living memory.

There was **arson** too. A reward of two guineas was offered for information on a gorse fire on High Lees in 1833. Sarah Kirk was given a £2–15s reward for apprehending Rowland Heathcote after he had set fire to Brough Mill in 1845. In 1863 there was a fire at Eastwood Farm, the property of Thomas Broomhead, with whose name we have become familiar.

Tobias Child's manufactory, Victoria Works down Mill Lane (today's holiday let was its shed) was set on fire in 1856. Mr Child had given up the Ordnance Arms by then and was living near his business. He got up in the night, and happening to look out of his window saw that the warehouse at the mill was on fire.

Hathersage
    May 8th 1856
At a Meeting of the Committee
of this Association concerning
the Fire at Mr Childs Manufactory
when it was resolved that the full
amount that our Rules will allow
namely 15 Guineas shall be offered to
any person as shall give such informa
tion as shall lead to the conviction
of the parties concerned in setting Fire
to the said Manufactory

The blaze spread very quickly because the nature of his business meant that the wooden rafters in the building were perpetually oil-soaked. Many of the villagers got up to help, bringing ladders and buckets. The warehouse and wire mill were abandoned to their fate, but the grinding mill and engine house were saved by dousing them with water from the Hood Brook.

The following publicity was placed in the Sheffield newspapers.

FIFTY GUINEAS REWARD.
INCENDIARISM.

Whereas some evil-disposed Person or Persons did, on TUESDAY NIGHT last, or early on WEDNESDAY MORNING, the 6th or 7th of May, 1856, MALICIOUSLY SET FIRE to the HACKLE and PIN and WIRE MANUFACTORY, belonging to Mr. TOBIAS CHILD, of Hathersage, doing Damage to the amount of £2500—

This is to give Notice, that whoever will give such information as may lead to the Conviction of the Offender or Offenders, shall receive the above Reward; Fifteen Guineas from the HATHERSAGE ASSOCIATION for the Prosecution of Felons, and Thirty-five Guineas from Mr. TOBIAS CHILD, of Hathersage.

Hathersage, May 8th, 1856.

There was good evidence of arson as there were sulphurous marks on the walls where an incendiary device had been thrown. Relations with the neighbours and the workforce were reported as cordial and no suspicion fell on the people of Hathersage, but three strangers seen in the village during the previous evening, had then disappeared. They were never traced, despite the maximum reward which was offered by Child's colleagues in the Association.

Mr Child had increased his stock-holding during Britain's recent war with Russia in order to keep his men working while trade was difficult. It was all destroyed by the fire and the damage was estimated as at least £2,500. Unfortunately, he had recently taken the decision to cancel the insurance on his premises as he considered his risks to be so low.

The manufactory eventually closed in 1910 after the steam boiler exploded. The word 'manufactory' is one of those splendidly descriptive words from the 19th century which, once abbreviated, was rarely to reappear in all its original glory, much like 'omnibus' and 'perambulator'.

Now to the matter of that mysterious manure mountain on page 42. The author calculates that the Association was undercharged by 2¼ pence (tuppence farthing). This translates to just under 1p, at a value of about 90p today. Mr. Marrison can, however, be forgiven for his oversight as he would not have had a calculator on his smart phone in 1883! Looked at another way, the Association got half a hundredweight of manure free of charge. Perhaps it was a bonus for buying what really was an awful lot of the stuff.

Prosecuting the Prosecutors

It is tempting to imagine that members of prosecution associations were pillars of their societies and whose characters bore no blemishes. Our libel laws compel me to say that this is indeed the case in the Association today. But the surprisingly litigious days of the 19th century meant that nobody was above prosecution.

Tobias Child frequently fell foul of the 1878 Factory and Workshop Act which stipulated employment conditions for children; he was successfully prosecuted on several occasions. And in the 1880s there were countless cases brought to Bakewell Petty Sessions against the Cooks for non-payment of wages. Godfrey Biggin, one of their Barnfield employees, applied to the court on no less than five separate occasions to secure his wages from the Cooks and each time he was accompanied by about a dozen co-complainants.

We will focus on three prosecutions: the first because it relates to a long-forgotten serious disturbance in Hathersage, and the other two because they reflect the realities of 19th century life in the village. The records of court proceedings enable the three stories to be recreated in some detail.

1.   Frost *vs* Cocker et al

When reading through the minutes of two hundred years of meetings, the records of 1831 stand out as the only reference to violent crime being dealt with by the Association, the main business of the prosecution associations being petty crime. The violent stuff, and there was plenty of it, was dealt with elsewhere and was outside the remit of the Hathersage Association. But the violence recorded in the 1831 minutes was perpetrated on members of the Association and their families, rather than on third parties, and makes for interesting reading.

It is said that there are two sides to every story, and these prosecutions clearly needed investigation beyond the boundaries of the Association records, but a read of the minutes from the committee meetings on the 1st of October and the 3rd of November 1831, is a good place to start.

By searching for details in the British Newspaper Archives several articles in the *Sheffield Independent* reveal the full facts of a dark event in the history of Hathersage, which deserve to be told in some detail. It transpires that the Association minutes did not give the full story and certain members of the Association may even have strayed onto the wrong side of the law.

Robert Cook, not yet a member of the Hathersage Association, had recently opened a factory in direct competition with the Cockers, who resented Cook's success and seem to have been looking for an excuse for conflict. Cook, an ill-tempered chap, had erected a house which obstructed an ancient carriageway and claimed that he had purchased the land. Samuel and Henry Cocker, both members of the Association, and Thomas Broomhead jnr, the village constable who would become a member a few years later, went and demolished the building on the 28th of September 1831. The villagers were outraged and allegedly burnt an effigy of Henry Cocker in protest.

1831 was a year of civil unrest in England. There were issues with the effects of the Corn Laws on prices, and with the recent

1831. ~~Oct 4~~ Octr 1st – At a meeting of
the Committee of the Fatherstage
Association for the Prosecution
of Felons &c held this day Octr 1st 1831
It was resolved – That in consequence
of some of the members of this Association
being threatened with great violence
by some person or persons unknown –
having fired Guns & Pistols & thrown
Stones &c against the House of one
of its members – and also a part of the
families & two of the members
having been assaulted by persons
known – It is therefore resolved
that a reward of £5.5.0 be paid
for the discovery of the ~~these~~ person or
persons threatening &c and that
warrants be immediately taken
out against the persons known

who have committed the
assaults – and that ~~the~~ ^the preson of Mr
Brewer be employed to
protect the interests of the
members of the Association
now alluded to

signed by – Samuel Birkbeck
J Swiff
Geo Morton
Wm Bremner

1831 ~~Sept~~ Oct 1st – At a meeting of
The Committee of the Hathersage
Association for the Prosecution
of Felons held this day Oct 1st 1831
It was resolved that in consequence
of some of the members of this Association
being threatened with great violence
by some person or persons unknown
having fired Guns or pistols & thrown
stones against the house of one
of its members – and also a part of the
families of two of the members
having been assaulted by persons
<u>known</u> – It is therefore resolved
that a reward of £5.5.0 be offered
for the discovery of the person or
persons threatening and that
warrants be immediately taken
out against the person known

who have committed the
assaults – and that if needful Mr Thos
Branson be employed to
protect the Interests of the
members of the association
now alluded to
signed by _   Samuel Cocker
                    N Swift
                    Geo Morton
                    Thos Broomhead

1831 Nov 3rd At a meeting
of the Committee of the
Hathersage Association for the
Prosecution of Felons held
this day — it was unanimously
resolved That in consequence
of an assault having been committed
upon Mr Henry Cocker by
James Lilliman and also
an assault having been
committed by George Fletcher
upon Mr James Morton, son
of one of the members of this
association _ that both the
said assaults be immediately
prosecuted to the utmost rigour
of the Law — signed by

       Saml Cocker
       Thos Broomhead
       Geo Morton

blocking of the Parliamentary Reform Bill. Rioting broke out in Derby, where a mob broke into the city jail and released some prisoners. The relevance of these riots to the events which unfolded in Hathersage a month later, is unclear, but it is possible that the village constable was feeling somewhat twitchy after this trouble elsewhere in the county.

At eight o'clock on the following evening, the two Cockers and Broomhead, the constable, were joined by Thomas Broomhead Sr, and the four of them went to confront Cook at the 'Ordnance Arms', where Cook was the tenant at that time. When they tried to get access, a melee ensued, during which a 40-year-old employee of Cook called William Frost allegedly struck out at the constable. He was arrested and dragged off to the village lockup.

The Lockup, courtesy of Heather Rodgers

The lockup was about a hundred yards down the road from the Ordnance Arms, tacked onto the side of the village hearse house. It had been built only three years beforehand, and paid for by the Duke of Devonshire in 1828. The photograph from 1938 shows the lockup addition on the side of an even older building, and how the whole structure had fallen into a sad state of repair by the time a tree fell onto it the day before the photograph was taken. The whole place needed to be demolished, and after years of serving different purposes, the location is now occupied by some high-class public lavatories. Several villagers, who couldn't resist taking part in the evening's activities too, tried to rescue Frost and they also got beaten up for their trouble. The prisoner was dumped on the bare floor of the cell with two large cuts in his head, his clothes soaked in blood and his body covered in scrapes.

That's when the first committee meeting of the Association took place, on the 1st of October. The minutes talk of guns being fired, rocks being thrown and, rather ominously, one of the local heavies being employed at the Association's expense "to protect the interests of the members". Samuel Cocker and Thomas Broomhead Sr were two of the four committee members that day.

Three weeks later, a Special Sessions was held at Hathersage in front of two Justices of the Peace. The location of the court is not specified, but the George Inn had been used for hearings in the past. Significantly, they used the word 'riot' to describe what had taken place. The allegation of assault by William Frost on the village constable was dismissed. A man called Smith claimed that he too had been assaulted by the constable, but witnesses testified that Smith had grabbed the constable's truncheon and thrown him to the ground before the constable had retaliated. Case dismissed.

Samuel Cocker was found guilty of assaulting two men

called Savage and Fretwell while they were trying to rescue their friend Frost. Cocker was fined a total of £3 and costs. A woman called Ann Smith claimed that she had been struck several times by Henry Cocker. A number of witnesses said that they were standing nearby and saw nothing of the sort, but she didn't deviate from her story when she was summoned to the Methodist chapel and questioned by the preacher. That was good enough for the magistrates; Cocker was found guilty and fined £1.

If all that sounds confusing and totally chaotic, it was. Dozens of witnesses were called during the day and the hearing went on until one o'clock in the morning.

The case of the main assault on William Frost went to the Derbyshire Easter Sessions in the following April. After another long day in court, counsel for the Cockers and Broomheads (all current or future members of the Hathersage Association) agreed to accept a guilty verdict. However, that still wasn't the end of it. When the guilty parties went for sentencing to the Derbyshire Midsummer Sessions, they decided to come out fighting and accused William Frost, Robert Cook (the tenant of the Ordnance Arms), two labourers called Higgett and Moseley, and numerous others, of riotous assembly on the 29th of September. They argued that the village constable had a duty to quell the riot and that he had called on his father and the two Cockers for help. Twice the court tried to persuade them to just sort it out between themselves for the sake of restoring peace in the village. On both occasions their counsels refused.

The cases for riotous assembly brought by the parish constable and the Cockers against William Frost and his friends were dismissed.

In sentencing the Cockers and the Broomheads, Lord Vernon adjudged that there had been 'irregularities' when Frost was taken without a warrant, but that these were mitigated by the 'tumultuous proceedings' going on around the accused men at the time. The defence counsel said some nice things about the Cockers, calling them very respectable and influential men who should be cleared of any opprobrium which had been thrown at them. The judge fined the Cockers and the Broomheads a token one shilling each. After all that!

None of these details is mentioned in the Association's minutes from the committee meetings of 1831 and 1832, nor does the event appear to have had an immediate effect on the guilty parties' membership status in the Hathersage Association, although in less than seven years Samuel and Henry Cocker had both resigned their memberships. Thomas Broomhead, the village constable, joined the Association two years after the riot and was a member until his death 46 years later. Sadly, it is not recorded whether Mr Thomas Bransom ever needed to be let off his leash to 'protect the interests' of the members under threat.

2.   Shuttleworth vs Cocker

Soon after resigning from the Association, Henry Cocker was back in court again, taken to Derbyshire Assizes in 1840 by John Shuttleworth, the member who lived at Hathersage Hall. Mr Shuttleworth was claiming damages for the 'effects of a nuisance arising from the defendant's needle manufactory'. John Shuttleworth employed a QC and two other lawyers who claimed that the dust and smoke from the works were soiling his laundry and that the noise from the extractor fans could be heard three miles away. Hathersage Hall had, of course, predated the mills. It is easy to understand Mr Shuttleworth's irritation, and that of residents employed in agriculture, at the racket and the filthy pall of dust and smoke which accompanied the arrival of the wire and needle industries. It was also in 1840 that Henry Cocker replaced waterpower with a steam engine at his Dale Mill, which was within 200 yards of Hathersage Hall. One can imagine the din and the smoke that this produced.

But if John Shuttleworth had a good point, so did Henry Cocker. He told the court that the fans were needed to protect his workers, two of whom had died in the previous month from 'grinders asthma' (silicosis). The disease itself not only considerably shortened life, it also predisposed the sufferer to tuberculosis. In his research, Christopher Side analysed the burial records of men from Hathersage in the 19th century and found that in 1840 the men who worked outdoors had a life expectancy of fifty-six, whereas for a metal worker it was a notable twenty years less. What is more, amongst those metal workers, the needle grinders were dying many years younger even than the wire drawers or needle hardeners; the particulate matter of metal and stone dust from needle grinding was lethal.

Henry Cocker had invented a form of extractor fan, powered by the main wheel in the mill, which drew the metal and stone dust up flues and blew it out of the building. But it had to go somewhere and instead of wrecking the respiratory systems of his employees, Mr. Cocker's invention enabled the dust and rust to settle on anything which was unfortunate enough to be within range.

The mill owner's legal counsel pointed out that the mill had been operating for ten years, yet Mr. Shuttleworth had never complained before, and they claimed that the real object of the action which Mr. Shuttleworth was bringing was to drive Henry Cocker out of the parish. This may or may not have been true.

The judge attempted to get Mr Shuttleworth to drop the case and come to some financial agreement with Mr Cocker to save himself the escalating costs of the prosecution, but he and his lawyers would not agree to do so. These were clearly litigious times. The verdict went in favour of John Shuttleworth, but he was awarded damages of only one shilling, equivalent to just £5 today.

Henry Cocker redesigned the extraction system so that the dust was diverted into the waters of the brook in the Dale, which would rightly have produced apoplexy in modern conservationists. But, at least, by 1900 the average age of death of metal workers and that of men working outdoors was similar, and both had risen to about sixty.

Meanwhile John Shuttleworth bought Nether Hall, a property by the river, to escape the foul air in the centre of the village, and although he enlarged and gentrified the modest homestead, he never actually moved to live there.

3. Marsden vs Cutler

We know from the letterheads which were reproduced in a previous chapter that at least two of the inns in Hathersage also rented out horses and carriages. We also know that they sold the resulting manure for 7s/6d a ton. In 1874, the landlord of the Ordnance Arms, James Marsden, hired out a horse and carriage to Rev Charles Cutler, the vicar of Hathersage, who was to become a member of the Hathersage Association five years later. An accident occurred, the carriage was written off, and the poor horse was so severely injured that it had to be destroyed. Mr. Marsden accused the vicar of dangerous driving and took him to court.

We have already come across the names of several landlords at the Ordnance Arms, and James Marsden is yet another. He had moved from Sheffield a few years earlier in order to run the inn. The forty-one-year-old Rev Cutler had been the Hathersage vicar for several years and was to remain in the job well beyond 1900. At the time of the accident, he had with him his wife, Julia, younger than him, and from South Africa, four daughters, and one son, all aged between one and ten years old.

It was on a summer's day that the vicar wanted to take his young family to a children's party in Eyam. He wasn't an experienced horseman and when he rented a horse and carriage, he usually also hired a driver, but on this occasion he decided to save some money by driving the carriage himself.

It was already getting dark when the family set off back home from Eyam to Hathersage. The route took them down Goatscliff, a notoriously difficult bit of steep track on the Eyam side of Grindleford Bridge. The horse was unfamiliar with the particular carriage which the vicar had hired and was rather large for it. Half-way down Goatscliff it became skittish, parted company from the carriage, bolted, and fell. Although his family escaped harm, Rev Cutler was dragged, badly injured, from the carriage by the bolting horse, and onto the road. He was unable to work for several weeks. The carriage was wrecked, and when a vet arrived the injured horse had already been taken off the track and into Booth's tannery yard in Grindleford (which was to become the laundry a few years later). The irony of the horse's premature relocation to the tannery was not lost on the jury and there was some stifled tittering until the judge showed his disapproval.

Mr. Marsden claimed that Rev Cutler was entirely to blame for the accident and demanded £50 compensation, worth about £5,000 today. He had bought the horse for 27 guineas and felt that the trap was worth at least £15. The vicar protested that he wasn't in the habit of driving recklessly, particularly with his family on board, and a series of witnesses were called who testified that the carriage was travelling at a walking pace when the incident happened. The jury believed the man of the cloth rather than the pub landlord and the case was dismissed.

This has been a turbulent chapter and it is nice to end it with good news. Unless, of course, you were the unfortunate horse.

Costs and Rewards

The cost of prosecuting the offender following a robbery at Thomas Cocker's property in 1821, was described in an earlier chapter. Members of the Association who suffered crimes first sought approval from the committee. They then just got on with it, organising the detection, arrest, and prosecution of offenders, totting up how much they were out of pocket at the end, and presenting an invoice to the Association's treasurer.

They were expected to squeeze as much money out of the county as they could before making their claim, and in 1810 it was felt necessary to define limits on some of the expenses which members could claim. Any wages were limited to two shillings a day, and the maximum allowance for hiring a horse was set at three shillings a day.

The chit on the next page, which was submitted to the treasurer in 1828 by George Morton, the landlord at the George Inn and one of the original members, after he was the victim of a robbery, shows that he claimed expenses for his sons William and James, and also for their horses. The bill doesn't specify what his sons had done to earn the money, but it does state that the parish constable was paid seven pence for supplying a letter. Son William was to take membership himself two years later and James became a member in 1841.

In December 1872, John Hibberson of Sickleholme had some ducks stolen. He ran the Marquis of Granby Inn and farmed fifty-four surrounding acres. The committee met on the 11th of the month and authorised Mr. Hibberson to 'prosecute the matter to the utmost extent at the expence of the Association'. He visited William Moore at Bamford Hall to seek his approval to obtain a search warrant. Mr Moore, the philanthropic member of the Association, who owned Bamford Mill, was a magistrate and was authorised to issue search warrants. Hibberson then needed to travel to Chapel-en-le-Frith to get the document.

The bill (shown on the next page) which Mr. Hibberson presented to the treasurer on the 14th, suggests that the daily allowance must have risen above two shillings by then, and he also included fees for the toll gates which he had to pass on his way to Chapel-en-le-Frith. He received his allowance at the annual dinner on the 26th of the month.

Sickleholme Decr 14th 1872
The Treasurer of Hathersage Association for
The Prossecution of Fellons
1872   To John Hibberson D^r
Decr 11th Jorney to Chappelenlefrith for
           search warrant by order of Mr Moore
           & the committee 10. 0
              Toll Gates .... <u>1. 6</u>
                                   11. 6
           Decr 26th 1872   John Hibberson

However, the amount offered by the committee did not always satisfy the claimant, as is shown in the note from William Johnston shown below. The minutes of the AGM in December 1893, which Mr Johnston did not attend, show that the members felt he had not tried hard enough when seeking an allowance from the county for pursuing the prosecution, nor had he provided enough information on how his expenses had been incurred. The Cowburn railway tunnel from Edale to Chinley had only been completed in March of that year and its ventilation shaft not finished until 1896, so the nature of the train journey for which he was claiming was not entirely clear. But he obviously considered the allowance '*much too Little*'.

Hathersage
Feb 20th 1894

Time Spent By W. Johnston in Prosecuting Ralph Miles
Septer 4th 1893 followed from Sickleholme
through Hathersage & drove to Chapelenfrith
Septer 6th drove to Chapele
then to New Mills
Allowed 15/- which I think is
Much too Little
William Johnston

The other factor which evidently irked the Association's subscribers was that Mr. Johnston was not even a member, but was an executor of John Cooper of Sickleholme, a member who had died eight years earlier. The executors of Mr Cooper's estate had never bothered to sell his share and seemed to be keeping the membership for precisely a situation such as this, where an offence was committed on the Sickleholme property, and they could make a claim.

The greatest expenditure of the Hathersage Association was in offering rewards 'for information which leads to the conviction of the person or persons responsible' for a particular misdemeanour. Five to fifteen guineas, at the discretion of the committee, was offered in cases of violent crime, theft of horses or horned cattle, and arson or robbery at a house, shop, warehouse, or mill. For stealing pigs, clothing or grain, and for robbery from outhouses or waggons, the reward was set at two guineas if the offence occurred in the day but three guineas if it happened during the night. Theft of coals or poultry, damaging walls or fences, and stealing fruit or vegetables, attracted a reward payment of one guinea for offences during the day and two guineas for those happening at night. It is interesting to see that offences committed at night were of a greater concern than those in the daytime. The rewards were always in guineas of course. For comparison, five shillings would have been a generous daily wage for a quarry worker in the mid-1800s.

The five occasions when the highest reward of fifteen guineas was offered occurred between 1845 and 1856. Those rewards were offered for solving crimes which involved breaking and entering, arson, and the theft of a lamb. The value of fifteen guineas at that time would have been equivalent to almost £2,000 today. On the other hand, the ten rewards which were offered between 1897 and 1927 were all pitched at two guineas, worth around £150 today, and several of those offences also involved the theft of livestock.

The recipients of rewards were asked to provide a receipt for their money, though few of these have been preserved. One which does survive relates to the theft of a single duck from Mary Cook in 1880. She was the wife of Robert Cook, the mill owner who lived at Barnfield House. The land around the house was not restricted by the railway line at that time and Mrs Cook dabbled in a bit of farming on the edge of the village.

A 13-year-old lad called Thomas Stanley was prosecuted for stealing the duck and in court he denied the charge, but William Crossland testified that he had seen Master Stanley throw his coat over the duck and make off with it. The court records state that the duck was worth 2s-6d and that it was eventually found dead. The value of the duck would not have made the Cooks' pursuit of justice worthwhile had it not been for their membership of the Association providing them with the funds. The magistrates directed that Thomas Stanley should receive twelve strokes with a birch rod, and the Association paid a one-guinea reward to William Crossland for going to court and providing the crucial information. The offence took place on the 2nd of July. The Association's committee met that same day and authorised financial support for the prosecution. The case was heard in court on the 16th and William Crossland signed a receipt for his one-guinea reward on the 21st. They certainly didn't hang about. All for a single duck worth half a crown.

At a meeting of the Committee held
this second day of July 1880 It was
stated by Mr Robert Cook on behalf
of Mrs Mary Cook that this day Thomas
Stanley of Hathersage had killed and
stolen a Duck and this was further
testified by William Crossland who
had witnessed the affair throughout
It was therefore agreed by the Committee
that the legal expences of the Prosecution
of the said Thomas Stanley shall be paid
by the Association and that after his
Conviction the Treasurer shall pay a
Reward of One Guinea to William Crosslan.

       Joseph R Cocker.

The one-guinea reward offered to William Crossland (above), and the receipt signed by him (below).

Hathersage
July 20th 1880

Received from the Chairman of the
Association for the prosecution of felons
the sum of one guinea for laying
information respecting.
    Thomas Stanley taking one
of Mrs Cooks ducks

£1··1··0   William Crossland

Between 1830 and 1927 the Association minutes record a total of fifty-two rewards being offered and the accounts show that they were claimed on thirty-five occasions, although other documents suggest that the real number must have been higher than this. Inflation would not have been a major consideration because from 1750 to 1900 the average annual inflation in Britain was only 0.4%. A reward of two guineas was offered in 1833 for information leading to the conviction of whoever set the gorse alight on High Lees, and in 1927 the same reward was offered for information on the damage to a property in Stoney Middleton belonging to Benjamin Thorpe (see below). In spite of the low inflation level, the first reward would be worth about £300 now, but the second would be worth less than half of that amount.

HATHERSAGE ASSOCIATION
FOR THE
PROSECUTION OF FELONS.
TWO GUINEAS REWARD
NOTICE IS HEREBY GIVEN
that the above Reward of

£2 2s. 0d.

will be paid to the person giving such information as will lead to the conviction of any person or persons displacing Stones from Walls, Damaging Fences, or any other Property in the occupation of Mr. B. THORPE, C.C., Riverdale, Grindleford.

Information to—

THE SECRETARY, Hathersage Association for the Prosecution of Felons.
BANK HOUSE, HATHERSAGE.

Greenup & Thompson, Ltd., Printers, Wellington Street, Sheffield.

On several occasions towards the end of the 19th century, members who had been the victims of crime topped up the rewards offered by the Association with a few guineas from their own pocket, and this added bonus was always mentioned on the posters which advertised the reward.

HATHERSAGE ASSOCIATION
FOR THE
PROSECUTION OF FELONS.
THREE GUINEAS REWARD.

Whereas some evil disposed person or persons did on the night of Thursday the 22nd, or early on the morning of the 23rd of December, 1881, feloniously break into the Fowl House of Mr. HUGH BRADWELL, of HATHERSAGE, and steal therefrom FIVE FOWLS. Notice is hereby given that the Treasurer of the above Association will pay the sum of Two Guineas and Mr. HUGH BRADWELL a further sum of One Guinea to any person giving such information as shall lead to the conviction of the Offender or Offenders.

J. R. BECKETT, PRINTER, 193, NORFOLK STREET, SHEFFIELD.

Hugh Bradwell (he signs himself Bradwall) was a very active member of the Association for forty-two years. Born in Offerton, he came to live at Cliffe House in Hathersage. He farmed 122 acres and as we will see, he was the parish constable for a time.

The 1840s and the 1890s were periods when a higher number of rewards were offered by the Hathersage Association, but this seems to have been a reflection of the zeal of the committee members rather than the amount of crime which was being committed in the Hope Valley at those times.

Neither does there appear to have been any pattern to the nature of crimes committed during those two decades, as is illustrated by the variety of offences which justified rewards when the committee met on September 4th, 1844.

1844

Sep 4th At a Meeting of the Committee of
the Hathersage Association for the
Prosecution of Felons it was agreed
to offer a reward of two Guineas on
the conviction of any person concerned
in the Mowing of Clover in the field
of Thomas Broomhead on Littlemore
on or about the 20th day of August
also it was agreed to offer a reward
of 2 Guineas to any person who shall
give information on the conviction
of any person who stole apples out
of the Garden of Mr Willm Morton
on or about the 28th of August
also to any person who shall give
information on the conviction of any
person that as been accustomed to
turn cattle into Grass belongin to Mr
Willm Morton

       Signd Wm Morton
           Thos Broomhead
           James Morton

It is interesting to note from the minutes and its transcript that the two victims of these three offences were both members of the sub-committee which authorised the rewards, so their enthusiasm may have been encouraged by self-interest.

Each time a reward was offered there was the additional cost of advertising the reward to consider. Such advertising in Hathersage was usually by means of handbills or billposting.

There are dozens of invoices from printing companies in the Association records and some of the surviving posters are reproduced in this book. The treasurer then paid 1s-3d to have each batch of 20 bills distributed around local villages. Other prosecution associations in Derbyshire made more use of newspaper advertising, which was usually more expensive but avoided the distribution costs. Just one association, in Retford, used a bellman or crier as the preferred means of advertising rewards. Between 1837 and 1861 that association paid for crying' on 61 occasions, at a cost of 1s-3d each time.

In its early days, the Hathersage Association occasionally also advertised in local newspapers. The Sheffield Mercury carried an advertisement in March 1820 to offer a reward following the sheep-stealing incidents at Grindleford Bridge, which were mentioned in a previous chapter. The invoice was for 8s-6d.

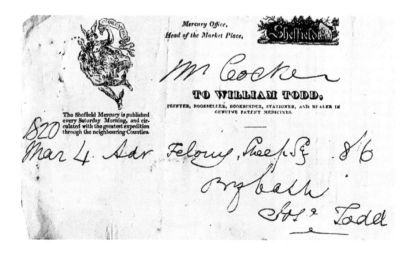

The committee also decided to advertise this same reward in another newspaper simultaneously, resulting in a second invoice a few days later with a similar charge for a newspaper entry. This second invoice includes a further 10s-0d for printing two hundred handbills. This is interesting as the newspaper is not named, but the bill came from someone called Montgomery. This was almost certainly James Montgomery, a famous Scottish-born hymn writer and poet, who had settled in Sheffield and published a radical newspaper called the Iris. That was presumably the publication in which the second advert appeared.

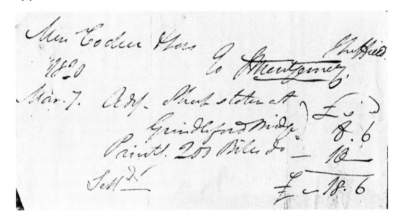

There had been a history of lead smelting on the North Lees estate before Joseph Ibbotson changed the industry to that of paper making in 1760. The paper mill was still in the Ibbotson family in 1820, when it was run by an Association member called Dennis Ibbotson. The strong brown paper which it produced was used for wrapping the products coming out of the Hathersage mills.

After a robbery at the mill, Dennis Ibbotson set about pursuing a prosecution following a promise from the committee to reimburse his expenses. So it was that, in July 1820, James Montgomery also gave Mr Ibbotson a bill for 7s-6d on a scrap of paper, requesting payment for an entry which advertised a reward in the Iris.

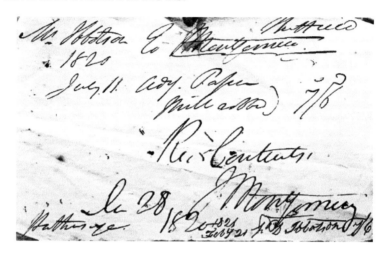

There seems to have been another indispensable element which formed part of mounting any successful prosecution, and which generated expense. At the end of each year, George Morton, the landlord at the George Inn where all the meetings were held at that time, would present a bill to the treasurer for the liquor which had been consumed by the committee members whenever they met to discuss a crime. The scrap of paper shown on the next page is the invoice for four meetings in 1819 and 1820, including those called to discuss the prosecutions of Matthew Kay, the sheep thief from Grindleford, and that of the paper-mill robber mentioned above (which the landlord refers to as the 'Ibbotson Affair').

Hathaway Dec 5 1820

The committee of the Hathaway
Association   Dr to George Morton

1819
June 9   For Liquors for when attending at post of Hospital $2.0
1820   Do Lectures
Do
July 8   Wine of Castor
            myself & Williams of fine

Settled in March 25 1839 Matthew Slay

The last mention in the minutes of a reward being offered or claimed was in 1932, when it is recorded that two guineas were collected "on behalf of Mr Shuttleworth". At the 1983 AGM there was a discussion regarding the re-introduction of the practice of offering rewards for information leading to convictions, but this seems to have been quietly forgotten. The nature of the Association, and of society as a whole, had moved on by then.

Other Tactics

Reading and interpreting the minutes of Association meetings was sometimes challenging. The level of the challenge varied between the capabilities of the holders of the post of secretary on the one hand (and there have been over twenty of them), and the nature of such writing implements as were available to members at the time, on the other. The steel-point pen was not patented in Britain until the 1820s and it is unlikely that the secretary would have progressed from using a quill until a few years after this patent was taken out. The fountain pen likewise was an invention from which the secretary would not have benefitted for several decades after that.

To demonstrate the author's difficulty, yet satisfaction, in reading the original documents, see the minutes from a meeting in 1833 on the next page. They were written using a quill. They also attest to the earliest subtle change of direction by the Association from the usual practice of simply offering 'rewards for information'.

Nicholas Swift, a member of the Association who lived in Outseats, had a silver snuff box which was stolen by Joseph Wainwright. Mr Swift successfully applied to the County Treasurer for an allowance towards the prosecution, but there was a shortfall of £2-7s-0d, which the Association paid. In addition to this standard payment by the committee, Edward Marsden was given a reward of £1, not for giving information leading to the prosecution, but for locating the stolen snuff box, and specifically for his honesty in returning it to Mr Swift. Joseph Wainwright was sent to Derby jail.

1833 Feb 27th
   Committee of the
At a meeting of the ^ Hathersage
Association, held this day, it was
resolved unanimously that Edward
Marsden be presented with 20/. for
his honesty in returning the stolen
property of Mr N Swift and
that this Association allow
Mr Swift all reasonable efficiency
for the prosecution of Joseph Wainwright
after he has first obtained all
that the County allow for the
prosecution of Felons – – – –
  Signed Saml Cocker

In 1867, four lads "committed depredations" on the property of Hugh Bradwall and they were summoned to appear in front of the committee. They were given the option of legal proceedings being taken against them or to cough up 1s-6d each to pay for the printing of handbills bearing an apology. They opted for the latter.

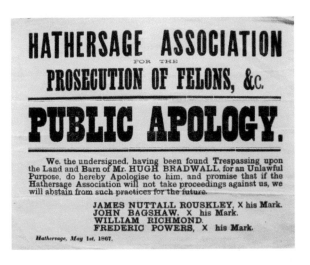

The police service had arrived in Hathersage well before 1871, and this was to generate an awkward situation which needed to be navigated. But on Saturday 11th March of that year, 21-year-old Thomas Richmond (brother to the William Richmond named in the above apology) stole a hat from John Hibberson's house. Mr Hibberson, you may remember, had an inn at Sickleholme and also farmed there. A meeting of the Association's committee was called for the Monday, at which payment to Mr Hibberson of the costs for legal proceedings were authorised and the village policeman was awarded two guineas for catching the culprit.

The Association's accounts show that the money for the reward was paid to the policeman five days later. Justice was swift, the policeman was happy, and Mr Hibberson got his hat back. Two guineas would have been a lot of money to pay for a hat in 1871. Let's hope it was a nice hat.

This represented another change in practice for the Association as it is the first recorded payment of a reward to the village policeman. Payments of rewards to police officers did not come to sit comfortably with the members, as we will see.

The 1861 census enables us to learn more about this troublesome Richmond family. The parents, James and Mary, had moved from near Redditch in Worcestershire, a town noted for needle making. They had their first child when James was twenty-seven and Mary was twelve. It is not clear in which Hathersage needle factory they worked when they arrived in Hathersage, but Robert Cook had moved to the village from the same area, so it may well have been the Barnfield Works. Thomas Richmond, the 21-year-old hat thief, had been eleven years old in 1861, and was already working as a 'needle spitter'. His brother William, the 20-year-old public apologiser, had been fourteen in the year of the census and was working as a 'needle eyer' like his mother.

The precise manual dexterity needed for needle making was considered beyond the capability of young people, but there were twelve children under the age of eleven listed as working in the Hathersage mills at the time of the 1861 census, and twenty-nine children aged between eleven and fourteen. This was significantly more than were involved in farming. Domestic work was the favoured job for young girls. There is good evidence that many children worked because they wanted to do so, rather than out of a need to earn money for their families.

The paper mill at North Lees, which had been owned by Dennis Ibbotson in 1820, was owned by James Marsden in 1873. This particular Mr Marsden had been a member of the Association since 1865 and was not the same James Marsden who as landlord at the Ordnance Arms had tried to get the vicar prosecuted for reckless driving.

When some windows were broken at the buildings of the paper mill by three local lads, the culprits, who were well known, were summoned to appear in front of the Association's committee. After personally apologising to Mr Marsden, the young men were reprimanded, and no further action was taken. The Association had effectively acted in a quasi-judicial manner and circumvented both the policeman and the magistrates.

It is interesting to note that, although Mr Marsden ran the paper mill, he lived at Furniss House on London Road in the village. The name of the house was later changed to Hawthorndene. Have you ever wondered what Station Road was called before the railway arrived? The Station Hotel, now the Little John, had been the Butcher's Arms.

In 1882, William Stanley was caught breaking the windows of a cottage in Bean Row on London Road; he too was summoned to meet with the committee of the Association. Annie Burrows came to the meeting to testify against Master Stanley as she had seen him in the act of breaking the windows. We now know where London Road was, and Bean Row was a terrace of cottages which ran between what is now the Little

John car park and the One Stop shop. The terrace was demolished in the 1930s to make way for council houses.

It had been William Stanley's brother Thomas who had stolen and killed one of the Cook's ducks in 1880 and had received twelve strokes with a birch rod after another lad had testified against him. We could reasonably infer that the Stanleys were a bit of a nuisance, and that they were neither sufficiently liked nor feared by other residents for them not to be grassed on. In any case, as the family were moving away from Hathersage a few days later, the committee members decided not to take the matter of the broken windows in Bean Row any further, although they felt compelled to inform the policeman of this decision. Because William Stanley never went to court and wasn't convicted, Annie Burrows was unable to collect a reward, which seems rather unfair.

About this time, the Association began to fund the production of signs and posters for use by its members. In 1894 Colonel Shuttleworth was troubled by people fouling his reservoir and throwing dogs into it. In addition to the offer of a one-guinea reward for further information, a notice board prohibiting such activities was fabricated and erected at the site of the reservoir at the expense of the Association.

Further signs were made in 1895 stating "Warning to Mushroom Gatherers and other Trespassers. Any person found gathering mushrooms or otherwise trespassing on land or property belonging to or in the occupation of the undermentioned will be prosecuted". These signs were underwritten with the names of all the members of the Association. Then in 1904 various "Trespassers will be

Prosecuted" posters were printed and distributed to members for display on their properties.

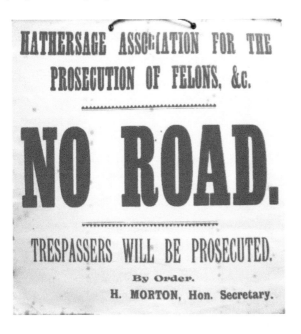

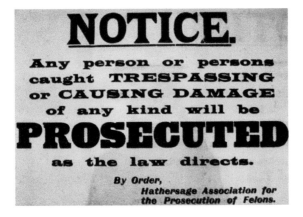

Courtesy of Heather Rodgers

On a few occasions the Association considered pursuing cases which did not directly involve its members. In 1904 "objectionable" graffiti appeared on the walls of the Hathersage church school and the committee was approached for assistance in catching the culprits. After looking into it further, the committee members decided that as the graffiti was *inside* the school it was up to the school managers to deal with it.

By implication, if the graffiti had been on the outside walls, it would have been a community problem with which they may have been willing to get involved. For example, following damage to the churchyard gates in January 1913, the committee decided to stray outside the normal practice of the Association and support a prosecution where the victim was not an individual member, but was the whole village community. The churchwarden had received complaints about the gates being left open and cattle straying into the churchyard, so he had bought good quality fasteners and had them fitted.

A few days later, as the congregation were arriving on Sunday morning, it was found that the fittings on the lychgate had been removed and stolen during the night. The damage would have required a crowbar, so the thieves must have come well-prepared. The committee offered a two-guinea reward for information leading to a prosecution. It was no coincidence that the church warden at that time was George Platts from Nether Hurst, a member of the Association, and it was he who wrote to his colleagues on the committee asking for the financial help. He had strong views on the thieves too.

NETHER HURST,
HATHERSAGE,
VIA SHEFFIELD.

Sunday night
Jany 19/1913

Dear Mr Butler

Some evil disposed person of persons has broken all the handles off the gates leading from the Eastwood end of the Church yard into the Church yard and they have taken some of them away

Mr Platts from Netherhurst explaining the damage for which he was requesting financial help

From Parish Constable to County Constabulary

We have already met the term 'parish constable', and been introduced to the activities of Thomas Broomhead, the Hathersage incumbent, on the turbulent evenings of 1831. The title goes back to the 13th century, but the system had undergone several changes before the formation of the Hathersage Association at the end of the 18th century.

The constables were given several duties in addition to that of bringing criminals to the courts. They monitored public houses, restrained loose animals, collected the parish rates, lit signal beacons, and caught rats. As this was all without a salary, they needed to continue their normal occupation at the same time. The constable had to be sworn into his job by the magistrates and the appointment usually lasted for one year. They had the right to read the Riot Act, though that doesn't seem to have happened in Hathersage in 1831.

The swearing-in ceremony that took place at Bakewell Petty Sessions in April 1855, would have been one of the last before the arrival of the police force. It was held before a bench of three members, which included the local MP and Lord Denman. The three constables who were sworn in for the Hathersage parish on that day were Hugh Bradwall (a familiar name), William Smith, a 54-year-old joiner, and a 30-year-old cattle dealer called Sebastian Smith. This neatly demonstrates the way that the constables overlapped with the prosecution association in Hathersage as the first two were already members of the Hathersage Association for the Prosecution of

Felons when they were inaugurated in 1855, and Sebastian Smith was to join ten years later. Constables for Outseats and Offerton were sworn in at the same sitting.

The constable would have regular communication with committee members when they were pursuing a prosecution for the Association. A chit from Thomas Cocker, reproduced in a previous chapter, shows that the fees paid to the constable and his men formed a significant part of the cost of any prosecution.

A note from the parish constable to the treasurer of the Association in 1806, requesting settlement for a payment, happens to have been written on the back of one of the constable's official forms which was designed for an entirely different purpose. While the constable's note is interesting, the blank and unused form on the other side of the piece of paper gives a fascinating insight into another of the constable's jobs. It may well be the only surviving copy of this document and is reproduced in full despite it not strictly being involved with a part of the prosecution process.

The form was designed for the constable to establish the details of every male living in Hathersage who was between eighteen and forty-five years of age. It is not a census. Although the earliest census in England had taken place in 1801, the first modern census did not occur until 1841. Neither is it a national form, as it was produced in Chesterfield. Men of these ages were compelled to join the Militia of the United Kingdom unless they had a good reason for exemption.

The militia was a military reserve for home defence, being used, among other things, to guard dockyards and prisoners of war. Because many of the regular soldiers were fighting overseas during the hostilities with France in 1806, recruitment into the militia had become a national priority due to a perceived threat of invasion by Napoleon's army. The militia regiments also acted as fertile recruiting grounds for the regular army.

To

TAKE NOTICE, That you are hereby required, within Two Days from the Date hereof to prepare and produce a List in Writing, to the best of your Belief, of the Christian Name and Surname of each and every Man resident in your Dwelling House, between the Ages of Eighteen and Forty-five, distinguishing in such List the several Particulars mentioned in the Columns thereof; and you are to sign such List with your own Name, and to deliver or cause the same to be delivered to me.

Dated the _____ Day of September, 1806.

Constable of

Name	Description	Age	Whether any Child, and if any, whether any under 14.	Exempt or not Exempt from Militia.	Grounds of Exemption.	Effective Volunteer or Yeoman.	Licensed Teacher not carrying on any Trade, or Enrolled Pensioner actually practising.

N. B. If any House is divided into distinct Stories, or Apartments occupied distinctly, each distinct Occupier is required to make this Return.

Neglect of Compliance with this Notice will subject the Party to a Penalty of Ten Pounds.

Take Notice, That the Twelfth Day of September, at the Hour of Ten in the Forenoon, at the White House is appointed for hearing Appeals within this Subdivision, by Persons claiming to be exempt from serving in the Militia.

Constable of

From 1757, an early form of conscription had been introduced. The parish constable had the job of constructing a *Militia Ballot List* with the names of all adult males. Ballots were then made from this list to decide who would actually serve for that parish. Men aged 18 to 50 were included from 1757, but in 1762 the upper age limit was reduced to 45. Certain occupations were exempt, such as judges, magistrates, constables, clergy, teachers, medical men, and apprentices. Family men with more than a certain number of legitimate children were not required to serve (before 1802 this was three children under ten, and after that men with any child under the age of fourteen). Any man under 5'2" tall or 'suffering under infirmities' was also deemed incapable of serving.

In each part of the county there would have been a local resident with some previous military experience appointed to command this somewhat reluctant band of men should their services become needed. Hathersage had the perfect commander in Ashton Ashton Shuttleworth, the Association member who lived at Hathersage Hall. Although he had given up his commission in the regular army a decade earlier, he had served with distinction in the war against the rebels in the American War of Independence. Consequently, he was chosen to command the local element of the militia. We are fortunate that the constable happened to scribble his note to the Association on the back of a spare form, and more than two centuries later we can see how the system for recruitment to the militia worked in North Derbyshire. Hostilities with France ceased in 1815, and in the 1820s all forms of military compulsion were abandoned.

By the middle of the century the role of parish constable was destined to change for ever. The Metropolitan Police was founded by Robert Peel in 1829 and ten years later the Rural Constabulary Act gave county magistrates the discretionary power to establish county police forces.

Opinions at the Derbyshire Quarter Sessions during 1839 were divided on the subject, there being a distinct difference of opinion between the more densely populated areas which favoured a police force, and the rural parishes which were against it. The argument primarily revolved around the cost to the ratepayer. The decision in Derbyshire went against the introduction of a county constabulary by a margin of twenty-nine votes to twenty-six.

Regardless, in 1856 the County and Borough Police Act mandated police forces onto those counties which had not adopted the previous legislation. Derbyshire had no choice, and Derbyshire County Constabulary was formed in March 1857. For some time, and in many areas, the new police force worked alongside the traditional parish constables, and the impact of this new entity was not immediate. With an initial strength of 156 men in the fledgling Derbyshire Constabulary, the policemen must have been thinly spread.

The activities of prosecution associations within Derbyshire show a gradual change in the types of offences with which they got involved. Some associations folded, but paradoxically, some new ones appeared. As the police took on a more active role in detecting and prosecuting serious offences, those societies which continued to function turned their attention to the type of offences in which they believed the police would not be interested. It was an uncomfortable period for the prosecution associations, during which their interface with the local bobby needed to evolve.

The first mention of a Hathersage policeman in the Derby Mercury was in July 1860, when Acting Sgt Hibbert prosecuted someone for cruelty to a horse. But Sgt Hibbert is not recorded in Hathersage in the following year's national census.

The previous chapter described the 1871 case of Hibberson's Hat, when the local policeman was rewarded with two guineas before there had even been time for a committee meeting to approve a reward, let alone to publicise one. That whole process was completed in a few days, without any record of a debate about the rights and wrongs of giving money to the policeman.

The original Hathersage police house, on Baulk Lane

In 1878, Police Sergeant James Martin caught William Ronksley (a cousin of one of the four miscreants who had been forced to issue a public apology in 1867) after he had broken into the house of Joseph Howell at Leadmill. Ronksley was twenty-five, came from Hillfoot, had previously been a game-keeper and had stolen some ferrets from Mr Howell's house. His name turned up frequently in the newspapers of the time, usually following a court appearance for poaching. He was a mirror image for the phrase 'poacher turned gamekeeper'.

The theft of ferrets was not a crime which attracted assistance from the county when pursuing a prosecution, so Mr Howell needed to pay the full 13s/6d for the expense of taking Ronksley to Bakewell, and 9s/6d in court fees. Ronksley was to get a month in Derby jail for his crime and the policeman claimed the reward which had been offered by the Association.

Mr Howell was only ever a member for two years because he moved back to live in Sheffield, but this case was to generate a controversy which the Hathersage Association's records describe as 'the Howell affair'. The decision to support Mr Howell was discussed at a committee meeting chaired by Tobias Child on the 6th of April. The Association had already committed to the costs of advertising a reward of two guineas, and the committee agreed to pay some of Howell's initial court costs, but after a long discussion they felt that it was beyond their authority to pay the reward to a policeman. The decision was deferred to the AGM at the end of December.

As the members began to express their disquiet, it became obvious that something had to change. Some felt strongly that policemen should have no right to claim rewards offered by the Hathersage Association as they were paid servants of the County. But other members thought that offering rewards to the local policeman might make him more vigilant in looking after the interests of the Association's members.

The committee sought the advice of John Taylor, a Bakewell solicitor. Mr Taylor pointed out that the wording in the Association's posters did not exclude police officers from claiming the reward, and that if they hadn't intended the policeman to claim it, the posters should have been worded differently. He charged 10s-6d for providing this advice.

Expenses of 10s-6d claimed by the solicitor

The chairman of the Hathersage Association wrote that, as *"the Police Force are well paid out of the County Rates, in future officers should only receive a reward of one pound and that the association's posters should be altered"*.

No decision to this effect was ever recorded in the minutes of the AGM, but the reward to Sergeant Martin was approved, if rather grudgingly (see page 103).

The fact that the policeman received his two guineas is confirmed by the receipt which he was asked to supply. It is written in his own flowing hand. The wording of subsequent posters never changed, but this was the last time that a policeman received a reward in Hathersage.

In 1888, a retired Derbyshire police inspector sued a prosecution association in Staffordshire for refusing to pay him a reward, but he was unsuccessful. Some Derbyshire groups ensured that the posters and newspaper adverts which offered their rewards explicitly excluded any entitlement of police officers, but that wasn't the case for the Hathersage posters. There was never an official police policy issued on this question of rewards and it appears likely that the relationships which developed between village policemen and their local prosecution associations were due more to the personalities of the people involved than to any official policy.

A Resolution was unanimously passed that Mr. Howell's Expenses be paid in the case of the prosecution of Poultby; also the Policeman reward of £3.2.0 be paid — the same time — the paid Proposed by Mr. O'Crocker. Seconded by Mr. Taylor. The Meeting think that part of the above expenses ought to have been paid by the County ——

Metamorphosis

W hen Hathersage Association for the Prosecution of Felons was formed in 1784 its sole purpose was to prosecute felons, but the 'Clubb night' soon became a social affair. The meetings took place at the houses of members, usually Joseph Marshall or George Morton (Mr Morton ran the George Inn, now the George Hotel). 'The book' was called at 8pm, which is when the business side of affairs kicked off.

When the meeting became an annual event in 1797, it was decided to provide a light supper at 6pm. It always took place in Christmas week. Any member arriving late for the supper forfeited sixpence, and those still absent for the official meeting at 8pm forfeited a further shilling. The food was initially just a minor addition to an evening of discussion about local crime.

The time of the annual get-together moved earlier in the day and by 1808 the supper had become a full-blown dinner which started at 2pm and took up the whole of the afternoon. It was referred to as the Annual Feast and had by then moved out of members' houses and into the George Inn. It can be seen from the inn's 1820 bill that each of the twenty members paid five shillings for their meal, which, despite providing a comprehensive range of refreshments, gave the Association a decent profit. The business part of the meeting still took place in the evening, by which time it is likely the members would have been fairly well oiled.

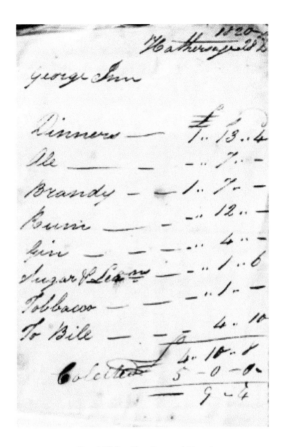

1820 bill for the Annual Feast

The 'fine' system for non-attendance at meetings or dinners described above continues to this day unless members have a very good excuse for their absence. It is difficult to think of a better reason than that given in 1839 by a lawyer called Thomas Gregory. He lived in Eyam and was due to come and give some legal advice to the members. The advice was with regard to the redrawn Articles of Association which are shown in Appendix ii.

The dinner was scheduled for the 26th of December and this letter was sent that morning to the Secretary, who lived at Leadmill. Mr Gregory is apologetic for his absence and goes on to offer his opinions on some of the issues which were going to be discussed at the meeting.

Eyam 26th Dec 1839

Dear Sir,

I grieve to inform you that I cannot have the Pleasure of attending your Association Dinner at Hathersage this Day as one of my Children now lies dead in the House _

Be pleased to present my Compliments & Thanks to the Gentlemen of your Association & say on any other Occasion I should have great Pleasure in joining them at Dinner

By the 1870s the fine for non-attendance at the annual dinner had risen to five shillings, the same as the cost for attending the meal. Despite this, the dinners were rarely attended by more than half of the members, but the members always delivered their apologies and payments promptly to the secretary to avoid the risk of exclusion from the Association.

Joseph Cocker's wire mill business at the Atlas Works was struggling in 1882 and he was approaching the end of his life. His letter of apology for his planned absence from the annual dinner that year, enclosing his fine, was written under the letterhead of Belle Vue, Hathersage. This was a house which he had had built, and to which he moved from Rock House so that he could be closer to his Atlas Works. Rock House is at the bottom of Church Bank, and Belle View was up Jaggers Lane, later to be renamed Sladen.

23 Dec 1882

Dear Sir

Neither myself, or Mr Ashton will be able to attend the Annual Meeting of the Association next Thursday I therefore send you 10/- the fines for not being there

Wishing you a happy Christmas and prosperous New Year

I am yours truly

Joseph R Cocker

Mr Broomhead

At the end of the 1800s, with a police presence well established in Hathersage, the business side of the annual meeting started to take a back seat and the Association began to allow members to bring other guests along to the dinner to boost the numbers at the meal. In an apparent attempt to raise the Association's profile, they frequently invited newspaper reporters from the Sheffield & Rotherham Independent and the Sheffield Telegraph. The reporters were even provided with bed and breakfast at the George Hotel at the Association's expense.

An edition of the Independent in 1898 carried a long article about the Hathersage Association, extolling its virtues and describing its 'ancient heritage', but barely mentioning the law enforcement aspect of its activities even though rewards were still being offered and prosecutions financed. When we consider the light-hearted cartoon which adorned the front of the dinner menu in 1908 (and continues to do so more than a century later) we can assume that the more formal side of Hathersage Association's existence must have been taken less seriously than in the previous century.

The dinners, almost always at the George Hotel until 1938, had become the most important feature of the Association. A 'dinner committee' was formed, its purpose being to set the menu and organise entertainment such as a *'humourist'*, a '*musical programme*', and even a '*demonstration of wireless*' on one occasion. With a reduced need to discuss crimes and organise prosecutions, food and entertainment took centre stage and the meal moved back to the evening. The capacity of the members for fine dining is illustrated in the following menu from 1909.

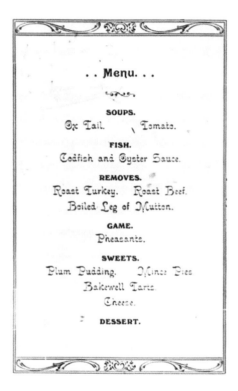

. . Menu. . .

SOUPS.
Ox Tail.   Tomato.

FISH.
Codfish and Oyster Sauce.

REMOVES.
Roast Turkey.   Roast Beef.
Boiled Leg of Mutton.

GAME.
Pheasants.

SWEETS.
Plum Pudding.   Mince Pies
Bakewell Tarts.
Cheese.

DESSERT.

The preparation of a bowl of punch to fuel the ever-increasing toast list was always an issue for discussion, with one member or another being tasked with the job each year. The bill for the constituents of the punch in 1897 suggests that the drink must have been potent. The minutes indicate that there were about fifteen attendees at the dinner that year. This was seventy years before the invention of the breathalyzer, and you could be reasonably confident that you and your trap would find the way home as long as the horse stayed sober. Goodness knows where all the cigars went.

. . Toast List. . .

1. "His Majesty the King and the rest of the Royal Family" .. .. The PRESIDENT.

2. "Army, Navy, and Reserve Forces" ..
   Rev. F. M. HAYWARD.

   Reply .. .. COLONEL SHUTTLEWORTH.

3. HON. SECRETARY'S REPORT.

4. "Hathersage Association for the Prosecution of Felons" .. .. Mr. R. H. DUNBAR.

   Reply .. .. .. The PRESIDENT.

5. "The New Members" .. Mr. H. R. CROSSLAND.

   Reply .. .. .. NEW MEMBERS.

6. "The President".. .. .. Mr. CURRY.

   Reply .. .. .. The PRESIDENT.

7. "The Visitors" .. .. ..Mr. TRUSTRUM.

   Reply .. .. .. Mr. R. H. DUNBAR.

8. "The Hon. Secretary and Treasurer"
   Mr. W. H. SWAIN.

   Reply .. .. Mr. T. T. CUTLER.

9. "The Host and Hostess" .. Mr. A. H. HAGUE.

   Reply .. .. The HOST.

There had been an extra dinner in 1887 to commemorate Queen Victoria's diamond jubilee and another in 1902 to celebrate the coronation of Edward VII. Then in 1915, following the outbreak of war, a decision was made to postpone the dinner indefinitely but for a five-strong committee to continue with the dwindling business of dealing with any crime occurring in the village during the hostilities.

After the Great War, the Association came back stronger than ever, with an increased appetite for fine food, good after-dinner entertainment and strong punch. The venue moved to the Scotsman's Pack and remained there for almost forty years. The fact that Albert Sunderland, the landlord, was a member of the Association, must have influenced that decision.

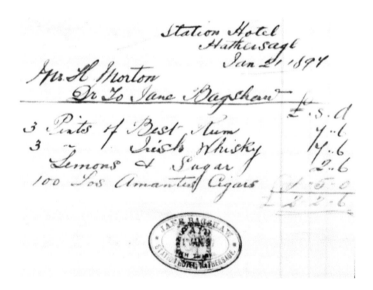

Constituents of the punch in 1897

- 112 -

The law-enforcement activities had ended in the 1930s and the Association had essentially become a dining club. At the outbreak of the Second World War, the reluctance to engage in anything which could be perceived as high living led to a cessation of annual dinners, and with no role to fulfil, the Hathersage Association went into hibernation for twelve years, a situation which had never happened since its formation in 1784 and was not to be repeated until the arrival of the 2020 Covid-19 pandemic.

When meetings restarted in the 1950s, the enthusiasm of the membership was undiminished. As if to confirm that the Hathersage Association had become a social gathering rather than a prosecutor of felons, a VIP guest was invited to the dinner each year: the Duke of Devonshire; the Master Cutler; the Chief Constable of Sheffield; the author L du Garde Peach, among others. Representatives from the other surviving associations in the area, such as those in Eyam, Baslow, Wentworth, and Norton, were invited to join Hathersage at their dinners from the 1960s.

The first occasion that the Association used its funds for something which may be described as a charitable purpose was at the initial dinner of the 20th century, on 11th January 1900. Now that a new century had dawned and the police were dealing with their previous mission, it was as if the membership sensed the need for another *raison d'etre*.

The minutes of the contemporary meetings oozed patriotism, and an awareness of things military which could almost be described as jingoism, and the first donation was to the Derbyshire Yeomanry. This was a part-time regiment which, in 1900, was equipping as a mounted infantry unit for service in the South African (Boer) War. At that same annual dinner, in 1900, the minutes record that a whip-round raised £1-14s-3d in appreciation of the entertainment after a visitor sang 'The Absent-Minded Beggar'. This song had been written during the previous year by Rudyard Kipling, and the music composed by Arthur Sullivan, for the sole purpose of raising money for a 'war fund' charity. The patriotic song caused a national sensation and was performed at events all over Britain throughout the Boer war. The 'Absent-Minded Beggar Fund' was sponsored by the Daily Mail and was the first recorded charitable project in support of a military conflict. Nationally, over the course of many months, it raised more than £250,000 for the families of soldiers who were fighting in Africa, equivalent to almost £30m today. The song clearly captured the spirit of the age and, as you might expect, there are renditions of it on YouTube for anyone interested in hearing it.

> As an amendment Mr. G. H. Cammell
> proposed and Mr. G. Platts seconded
> That the five pounds be given towards
> the fund for the equipment of the Derbyshire
> Yeomanry -- Carried.
> After the singing of Mr. Rudyard Kipling's
> song "The Absent Minded Beggar"
>   by Mr J.G.Lister the sum of 1.14.3
> was collected for "Daily Mail War Fund"

Only sixteen years earlier, when the bank balance had risen to £71, the members were each given £1 from the funds as it was felt that the amount of money in the Association was too high. At that time there were no thoughts of donating any surplus funds to charity. The fact that the George Inn charged 5s a head for the annual dinner puts this £1 'cashback' into perspective.

There are no further records of charitable donations for a century. In 1988 a raffle started to be held at the annual dinner, and this caused the bank balance to rise rapidly over the next ten years.

A decision was made at the AGM in 2,000 to donate £200 to a victim support organization. This seems to have set the future course for the Hathersage Association, and since then, donations of gradually increasing sizes have been made to locally based charities. By then, times had changed. The Derbyshire Constabulary had arrived, and this completed the metamorphosis from a prosecution association to a charitable organization.

Epilogue

Hathersage Association for the Prosecution of Felons was one of many similar organisations in England which sought to deter and prosecute minor crime before a police service existed. The national network of prosecution associations provided an insurance-based approach to the high expenses involved in private prosecutions, but only for the benefit of those who were inclined to join an association and could afford to do so. If the state mechanism was failing to protect them from the minor types of crime, then the people who could afford to join such groups were determined to protect themselves.

These organisations represented local initiatives which brought first-hand knowledge of the area and a localised, pragmatic approach to law enforcement and prosecution. Examining the detailed records of the Hathersage Association provides an insight into the extent of minor criminal behaviour and how it was handled, both before and after the existence of the local policeman.

The transformation of prosecution associations into purely social gatherings took 150 years to happen, a process inevitably accelerated by the development of a paid police force. Perhaps surprisingly, the change was not immediate upon the arrival of the police, and those associations which survived the change seem to have adopted a quasi-judicial role for a few years, dealing with petty offences without necessarily involving the police or the courts. Since the early decades of the 20th century, the transformation into groups focused on conviviality, and more recently on raising money for local charities, has been complete. Only the quaint-sounding names betray their history.

That change in nature of the prosecution associations could be seen as marking an end to the formal interaction between local communities and the criminal justice system. This interface did not truly return until the introduction of community-based policing initiatives such as Neighbourhood Watch in the 1960s.

It should be remembered that the catalogue of crimes which are documented in the Hathersage Association's records includes only those offences which directly affected that handful of people who happened to be members of the group. The true level of offending is likely to have been higher.

Clearly, rural crime and antisocial behaviour are not new phenomena and have been a constituent of life as long as communities have existed.

Appendix i

First Page of the Original Articles of Agreement
(20th March 1784)

Appendix ii

First Page of the Redrafted Articles of Agreement
(18th January 1838)

Articles of Agreement Intended made concluded and fully Agreed upon the Eighteenth Day of January in the year of our Lord One Thousand eight hundred and thirtyeight Between William Morton of Lead Mill in the Parish of Hathersage and County of Derby Miller an Butcher, Henry Cocker of Hathersage aforesaid Mill Drawer, Charles Hobson of Greens House in the Parish of Hathersage aforesaid Farmer, Thomas _ _ _ Broomhead Junior of Hathersage aforesaid Shoe Maker of the one Part and Henry Broomhead of Hathersage aforesaid Shoe Maker of the one Part and All and every those other Persons whose Names are hereunto subscribed and Seals affixed of the other Part as followeth.

Whereas divers Felonies Larcenies Robberies have lately been committed to the great Damage and hurt of Honest and Industrious Persons and such Transgressors too often go unpunished by reason of the Costs and charges attending the Prosecution of such Persons as are guilty of such Felonies Larcenies or Robberies or by reason of some Private Agreements made to prevent Prosecutions for such Offences Now these Presents Witness that to the Intent that such Offenders may be brought to Public Justice We do hereby Covenant and contracted and agreed upon by between and amongst us whose Names are hereunto subscribed and who have signed and sealed these presents and each and every of us do hereby for our own parts respectively and for the one for the other of us Covenant promise and agree to and with each other of us whose names are hereunto subscribed and sealed as by these Presents in manner and form following. First it is hereby agreed that if it shall happen that anyone or more of us whose Names are hereunto subscribed and sealed shall have any of our Horses broken or Goods or Cattle (or our own Custody or keeping even the Custody or keeping of any of our Servants) stolen that such Offender and Offenders shall be prosecuted for such Offence and Offences by us whose Names are hereunto subscribed and sealed at our joint and equal Expense without any regard to be had to our Quantities or the quantity of our Estates. And it is hereby

Appendix iii

Historic Membership and Years Active

Henry J Ibbotson	1784 - 1797
George Morton	1784 - 1834
Richard Oliver	1784 - 1809
Thomas Furniss	1784 - 1809
John Wilcockson	1784 - 1806
Thomas Hadfield	1784 - 1834
Samuel Ibbotson	1784 - 1818
John Gardiner	1784 - 1793
Joseph Marshall	1784 - 1802
James A Shuttleworth	1784 - 1795
Robert Cocker	1786 - 1802
William Eyre	1786 - 1834
Joseph Ibbotson	1786 - 1844
Mary Ibbotson	1786 - 1818
Thomas Walton	1786 - 1819
Rev Powell	1791 - 1799
Chris Kirk	1791 - 1822
Thomas Marshall	1791 - 1797
Ashton A Shuttleworth	1796 - 1830
Thomas Cocker	1796 - 1834
William Ibbotson	1797 - 1842
Thomas Ibbotson	1802 - 1812
Thomas Worrall	1806 - 1836
Joseph Brocklehurst	1806 - 1828
John Furniss	1806 - 1830
Dennis Ibbotson	1806 - 1828
Henry Cocker	1809 - 1838
Samuel Oliver	1809 - 1822
Thomas Broomhead	1809 - 1842
James Furniss	1809 - 1833
Henry Ibbotson	1819 - 1834
Samuel Cocker	1819 - 1836
Hannah Ibbotson	1819 - 1830
Joseph White	1820 - 1834

Nicholas Swift	1828 - 1837
Charles Ibbotson	1828 - 1867
John S Ashton Shuttleworth	1830 - 1894
William Morton	1830 - 1844
Henry Thorp	1830 - 1844
Robert Cocker	1831 - 1834
George Eyre	1834 - 1883
Thomas Broomhead Jr	1834 - 1880
Benjamin Kirk	1836 - 1842
William Thorpe	1836 - 1878
Henry Broomhead	1836 - 1849
Thomas Brightmore	1836 - 1842
James Robinson	1838 - 1847
James Morton	1841 - 1865
Sarah Kirk	1842 - 1845
William Tomasson	1843 - 1853
Tobias Child	1844 - 1889
Hugh Bradwall	1844 - 1886
Robert Cook	1844 - 1867
George Morton	1845 - 1861
Benjamin Grayson	1846 - 1864
Charles Robinson	1847 - 1867
John H Bradwell	1847 - 1853
Anthony Farnsworth	1847 - 1857
William Smith	1849 - 1857
John Bagshaw	1850 - 1864
John Hibberson	1853 - 1880
Joseph Cocker	1856 - 1883
George Barker	1860 - 1884
Thomas Sayer	1863 - 1891
Robert Howe Ashton	1864 - 1886
William C Moore	1864 - 1888
James Marsden	1865 - 1885
Dr Joseph Henry Taylor	1865 - 1897
Mary Robinson	1867 - 1877
Abraham Ibbotson	1868 - 1872
Richard Cook	1868 - 1877
James Cook	1869 - 1877
Charles Cammell	1869 - 1879

Benjamin Smith	1870 - 1888
John Cooper	1872 - 1885
Joseph Crossland	1875 - 1818
Robert Cook	1877 - 1890
John Robinson	1877 - 1913
Charles E Marrison	1878 - 1898
George H Cammell	1879 - 1905
Rev Charles Cutler	1879 - 1892
Joseph White Broomhead	1880 - 1890
William Eyre	1880 - 1896
James Benton	1882 - 1890
J.M. Haslam	1883 - 1893
George Cooper	1883 - 1907
Henry R Crossland	1883 - 1933
William Wallworth	1888 - 1903
Henry Morton	1889 - 1924
John Bateman Bagshaw	1890 - 1899
John Francis Cook	1892 - 1902
Thomas T Cutler	1892 - 1925
George Platts	1883 - 1914
Richard Jennison	1893 - 1920
Col Ashton J Shuttleworth	1894 - 1913
Alfred Trustrum	1896 - 1910
W H Swain	1896 - 1917
William B Wolstenholme	1896 - 1900
Mark Spittlehouse	1897 - 1915
Dr Herbert Graham Lander	1897 - 1917
Hives Barber	1897 - 1904
Maj J H Leslie	1898 - 1902
Elizabeth A Walker	1898 - 1907
J B Asterley	1898 - 1910
William H Ibbotson	1898 - 1907
Lorenzo Youle	1902 - 1906
Arthur E Marsden	1902 - 1907
Waldo E Mawhood	1902 - 1915
Ashton A. Shuttleworth	1903 - 1914
James E Webster	1904 - 1920
Edmund J A Shuttleworth	1904 - 1907
Benjamin Thorpe	1905 - 1952

Ambrose Frith	1906 - 1914
T Gifford Elliott	1907 - 1914
A H Hague	1907 - 1913
William Thompson	1907 - 1914
Harvey Foster	1907 - 1920
Samuel Ellis	1908 - 1914
W Abbott	1908 - 1915
H J Price Jones	1910 - 1918
R. Wardrobe	1911 - 1934
Maj Leonard E Colley	1913 - 1932
Thomas Dobb	1913 - 1920
Percy J Turner	1913 - 1952
T H Brown	1914 - 1931
Alfred Ridge	1914 - 1925
Thomas Spittlehouse	1915 - 1920
H Lloyd Jones	1915 - 1920
B M Heald	1918 - 1933
Charles P Marrison	1918 - 1952
G E V Wood	1920 - 1926
E A Holmes	1920 - 1923
Arnold Roberts	1920 - 1923
Col A W Chadburn	1920 - 1939
J L Cockayne	1921 - 1932
Dr William Houlbrook	1921 - 1939
Earnest E Scott	1921 - 1937
John Swindell	1923 - 1952
John William Froggatt	1924 - 1927
Maj Gregory G Rose-Innes	1925 - 1937
Samuel R Crossland	1925 - 1961
Tom Owen Froggatt	1927 - 1939
Albert Sunderland	1931 - 1952
Col Francis Colley	1932 - 1954
F W Scorah	1932 - 1939
Aaron Hancock	1933 - 1939
Robert Thorp	1933 - 1962
Frederick Wardrobe	1934 - 1974
John Arnold Roberts	1937 - 1965
John Ashton Shuttleworth	1937 - 1984
Alfred Chadburn	1939 - 1966

George Mellor	1952 - 1967
George Gibbins	1952 - 1972
Benjamin Rowland Thorpe	1952 - 1982
Percy Wardrobe	1952 - 1971
Peter Roberts	1952 - 1967
Harold Sunderland	1952 - 1967
R Turner	1952 - 1970
Max Cockayne	1952 - 1980
Robert Crossland	1952 - 2001
William Watson	1952 - 1984
Joseph Dalton	1953 - 2004
Col Bob Craig	1953 - 1960
J B Rowarth	1953 - 1974
Ralph Firth	1954 - 1961
Eddie Caudwell	1954 - 1982
Joe Hartle	1954 - 1974
Charles Furness	1954 - 1997
Hugh Cameron	1956 - 1984
John Thorp	1956 - 1963
Robert Marsden	1957 - 1983
Peter Crossland	1961 - 2002
Ray Ollerenshaw	1962 - 1994
J R A Bull	1965 - 1971
Arthur Elliott	1966 - 1983
Michael Shuttleworth	1967
Cyril Dalton	1967 - 1991
Ken Grayson	1967 - 1983
Joseph Ibbotson	1969 - 1994
E J Smith	1970 - 1981
Philip Cox	1971 - 2003
Stuart Ollerenshaw	1971 - 2004
Ray Platts	1972 - 2016
Joe Rowarth	1974 - 1990
Tommy Wreaks	1974 - 1983
Joe Dalton	1979 - 2004
Jack Weaving	1980 - 2012
Rowland Thorpe	1982
George Elliott	1982
Sandy Caudwell	1983

Stuart Elliott	1983
Percy Hassall	1983 - 1997
Doug Paget	1983 - 1999
Edward Marsden	1984 - 1991
Robert Watson	1984
Mark Latimer	1984 - 2014
Maurice Wilson	1990 - 2015
Tony Palmer	1991 - 2012
Geoff Eyre	1991
Graham Cooper	1992
Nigel Dalton	1994
George Platts	1995
Maurice Cottrill	1996 - 2007
Malcolm Robinson	1996 - 2008
John Crossland	1996
Tony Doyle	1997 - 2016
Dr David Moseley	1997
John Hall	2002 - 2015
Stuart Ollerenshaw Jr	2004
Peter Eyre	2004
Edward Caudwell	2005 - 2018
John Cottrill	2007 - 2020
Ron Priestley	2008 - 2012
Tony Priestley	2011
David Priestley	2012
Tony Favell	2012
Alan Furness	2012
John Wain	2014
Philip Cresswick	2015
Brian Wilson	2015
John Platts	2016
Nick Williams	2016
John Morley	2018
Matthew Cottrill	2021

Appendix iv

A Map of Hathersage in the late 19th Century

(For most of the century, the southern part of the village was not sliced by the railway line)

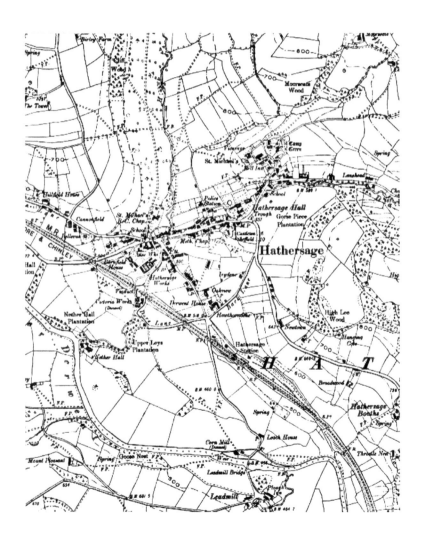

1. Dale Mill
2. Hathersage Hall
3. Ordnance Arms
4. Village lockup
5. George Hotel
6. Atlas Works
7. Bocking's shop
8. Barnfield (Hathersage) Works
9. Victoria Works

Printed by: Copytech (UK) Limited trading as
Printondemand-worldwide.com
9 Culley Court, Bakewell Road, Orton Southgate,
Peterborough, PE2 6XD